MARGARET SILF

W9-AVR-787

# 2012

## A BOOK OF GRACE-FILLED DAYS

LOYOLA PRESS.
A JESUIT MINISTRY
Chicago

LOYOLA PRESS.
A JESUIT MINISTRY

3441 N. Ashland Avenue
Chicago, Illinois 60657
(800) 621-1008
www.loyolapress.com

*Cover and interior design by Kathy Kikkert*

**Library of Congress Cataloging-in-Publication Data**
Silf, Margaret.
  2012 : a book of grace-filled days / Margaret Silf.
    p. cm.
  ISBN-13: 978-0-8294-2912-1
  ISBN-10: 0-8294-2912-3
1. Devotional calendars—Catholic Church. 2. Catholic Church—
Prayers and devotions. I. Title.
  BX2170.C56S5612 2012
  242'.2--dc22

                                        2011014945

Printed in the United States
11 12 13 14 15 Bang 10 9 8 7 6 5 4 3 2 1

# INTRODUCTION

I once heard a funeral homily that made a deep impression on me. Actually, it wasn't the homily so much but just one comment the pastor made. He remarked that we usually remember people, at least in the inscriptions on their tombstones, by the year of their birth and the year of their death. What really matters, he added, is the dash in between—that little dash, an insignificant punctuation mark connecting two significant dates. In God's eyes, though, that dash is important. It isn't the start and end dates of our time on earth that matter but what we do with the dash in between.

These thoughts led me to ponder how I see my own life. Perhaps I tend to think of my life as a kind of package, wrapped up between its start and end dates, to think that I have to "get myself together" in order to present something acceptable to God when I arrive at the pearly gates. The pastor's words shifted my perspective. Now I see my life more in terms of the open conduit or pipeline through which the Holy Spirit is longing to flow, potentially transforming, through God's grace and power, the various situations and circumstances that I encounter. When and where that conduit begins and ends isn't important. What matters is that I don't block it up with too much of myself and my concerns and obstruct the free flow of the Holy Spirit. His words also reminded me that my own bit of the conduit is just a segment, albeit a unique and indispensible segment, of the conduit of all humanity, through which God is longing to flow.

We are standing once again on the threshold of Advent, a new year. Advent reminds us, sometimes quite forcibly, of the approaching winter and the approaching "end times," but above all, Advent calls us to prepare and to listen for the coming of Emmanuel—God-with-us. Emmanuel invites each one of us to allow the Holy Spirit to flow through our daily lives. All too easily the dash becomes a frantic dash to pack in too much activity and become clogged with our self-importance. I remember, for example, when I first left corporate life in the computer industry to spend more time writing and reflecting, I would sometimes think back to my days in the office, the urgent meetings, the dizzy deadlines, and wonder *What was all that about?* It doesn't take too many months of having hindsight to bring a different perspective to all the feverish urgency of our working lives.

"But it's not that simple," you might say. The tasks that get us into a spin do have to be done. The children do have to be fed. The deadlines do have to be met. How could we begin to respond, then, to the Advent promise of our God to be God-with-us? How might we begin to honor the ever presence of God in the hours and minutes of life?

Jesus wasn't immune to this problem. Very often, we learn, he found himself besieged by the demands of a hungry throng, desperate for his attention and his action. And just as often, we learn that he took himself off to a quiet place to be with the Father, to draw on the source of all his power, so that Jesus' life became an incarnation of what it means to be wholly with the God who is wholly with us.

This little book is an invitation to you to follow this example and to take just a little time out during each day simply to be in the presence of the One who is constantly with *you*. You don't need to take off into the desert, physically. Such opportunities simply don't present themselves in the normal workaday world. But most people can find a few minutes, somewhere and at some time during a busy day, just to be alone in their hearts with God. To help you focus your heart more deeply on God in those moments, this book offers you a fragment of Scripture each day, selected from the lectionary readings for the day. Let the words from Scripture take root in your heart. The reflections offer a thought for the day and are intended to help you discover your *own* thought for the day and to notice how the meaning of the Scripture connects to the things that are going on in your life.

God speaks to us through God's word, if we take the time to be still and to listen. But God also speaks to us in and through the moment-by-moment reality of our experiences. May these daily words and thoughts help you connect the two and may they become gateways of grace for you, wherever you are and however your life runs its daily course. May the year ahead be blessed and made fruitful by the time you spend with God, who is waiting, even now, to become incarnate in your world.

*No ear has ever heard, no eye ever seen, any God but you
doing such deeds for those who wait for him.*

—ISAIAH 64:3

As a new year approaches, may we, like newborn babes
in a new place, open our eyes and ears, as if for the first
time. May we greet with open hearts the good news that is
coming to pass.

Isaiah 63:16–17, 19; 64:2–7
Psalm 80
1 Corinthians 1:3–9
Mark 13:33–37

---

*Monday*

# NOVEMBER 28

*In days to come,*
*The mountain of the LORD's house*
*shall be established as the highest mountain*
*. . . All nations shall stream toward it;*
*many peoples shall come and say:*
*"Come, let us climb the LORD's mountain,*
*to the house of the God of Jacob,*
*That he may instruct us in his ways,*
*and we may walk in his paths."*

—ISAIAH 2:2–3

Perhaps the mountain has a name: the moral high ground.
No nation has the right to claim it, but the One who is
coming makes a home there and will draw all of us closer
to its sacred slopes.

Isaiah 2:1–5
Psalm 122
Matthew 8:5–11

⇒ 2 ⇐

*A shoot shall sprout from the stump of Jesse,*
*and from his roots a bud shall blossom.*
*The Spirit of the LORD shall rest upon him:*
*a Spirit of wisdom and of understanding,*
*A Spirit of counsel and of strength,*
*a Spirit of knowledge and of fear of the LORD.*

—ISAIAH 11:1–2

This is no hesitant spirit, no shy retiring violet, but a surge of life-transforming grace pushing out from the ancient root of our sacred story. This spirit will bear new fruit, new ways of thinking and relating, a fresh wind in the universe.

Isaiah 11:1–10
Psalm 72
Luke 10:21–24

---

*As Jesus was walking by the Sea of Galilee, he saw two brothers,*
*Simon who is called Peter, and his brother Andrew, casting a net into*
*the sea; they were fishermen. He said to them, "Come after me, and I will*
*make you fishers of men."*

—MATTHEW 4:18–19

I wandered along the beach in northeastern Scotland,
where my family has its roots, and listened to the local
fishermen talking to one another in their broad dialect.
These were men toughened by a hard life at sea, men who
knew what life is truly about. I imagined what they would
have made of Jesus' call and marveled at the magnetic
power of this man who can attract instant allegiance, even
across thousands of years, from the toughest and most
skeptical hearts.

Romans 10:9–18
Psalm 19
Matthew 4:18–22

———————

≥ 4 ≤

# DECEMBER 1

*Open to me the gates of justice;*
*I will enter them and give thanks to the LORD.*
—PSALM 118:19

It always takes me by surprise that when the gates of
holiness open, however briefly, they usually reveal not
some distant castle in the sky but our own backyard. Holy
gates invite us to discover God right here.

Isaiah 26:1–6
Psalm 118
Matthew 7:21, 24–27

# DECEMBER 2

*The LORD is my light and my salvation;*
*whom should I fear?*
*The LORD is my life's refuge;*
*of whom should I be afraid?*
—PSALM 27:1

When I walk in God's light, I don't need to fear whatever
may be lurking in the darkness.

When I lean back on God, I don't need to fear whatever
may be standing in front of me.

Isaiah 29:17–24
Psalm 27
Matthew 9:27–31

*Without cost you have received; without cost you are to give.*
—MATTHEW 10:8

We come into this world with nothing but God's abundant gifts. All we can add to them is our own price tag. Doesn't that bring up some questions about the honesty of our accounting?

Isaiah 30:19–21, 23–26
Psalm 147
Matthew 9:35—10:1, 5a, 6–8

# DECEMBER 4

*Make straight in the wasteland a highway for our God!*
*Every valley shall be filled in,*
*every mountain and hill shall be made low;*
*The rugged land shall be made a plain,*
*the rough country, a broad valley.*

—ISAIAH 40:3–4

God is the great leveler. This work may involve much more than smoothing out the mountains of difficulty and the valleys of despair. It may also mean leveling down the mountains of all-consuming prosperity to fill the gaping emptiness in the valleys of poverty.

Isaiah 40:1–5, 9–11
Psalm 85
2 Peter 3:8–14
Mark 1:1–8

*Strengthen the hands that are feeble,*
*make firm the knees that are weak,*
*Say to those whose hearts are frightened:*
*Be strong, fear not!*
—ISAIAH 35:3–4

The irony is that we cannot hear these encouraging words
and take them to heart until our hands are weary, our
knees are trembling, and our hearts are faint. Only then do
we understand the power and love behind those actions.

Isaiah 35:1–10
Psalm 85
Luke 5:17–26

*What is your opinion? If a man has a hundred sheep and one of them goes astray, will he not leave the ninety-nine in the hills and go in search of the stray?*

—MATTHEW 18:12

The television news broadcasts an appeal for a missing child. The local police force, the entire neighborhood, and all the friends and family are out searching. Those who love the little one will search ceaselessly for as long as it takes, for a lifetime if necessary. If we care that much, what can we say about God?

Isaiah 40:1–11
Psalm 96
Matthew 18:12–14

*Wednesday*

# DECEMBER 7

*He does not faint nor grow weary,*
*and his knowledge is beyond scrutiny.*
*He gives strength to the fainting;*
*for the weak he makes vigor abound.*

—ISAIAH 40:28–29

The One with unlimited understanding and boundless energy wants nothing more than to give it away to us, who have nothing.

Isaiah 40:25–31
Psalm 103
Matthew 11:28–30

⇒ 11 ⇐

*Mary said, "Behold, I am the handmaid of the Lord. May it be done to me according to your word."*

—LUKE 1:38

When the Spirit hovers over our hearts, we have two choices: to resist and close down or to give our unconditional consent for God's dream to come to birth in our lives. There is no halfway position. It's not possible to be only a little bit pregnant.

Genesis 3:9–15, 20
Psalm 98
Ephesians 1:3–6, 11–12
Luke 1:26–38

*If you would hearken to my commandments,*
*your prosperity would be like a river,*
*and your vindication like the waves of the sea.*

—ISAIAH 48:18

It's important to remember what might have been, but only as an aid in learning from the past, so that we can make a different kind of future.

Isaiah 48:17–19
Psalm 1
Matthew 11:16–19

---

*Blessed is he who shall have seen you*
*and who falls asleep in your friendship.*
—SIRACH 48:11

Does that seem to rule you and me out of the running?
We haven't seen God—or perhaps we have: in the daily
miracles that lie everywhere around us. We haven't died
yet—perhaps we can, at the end of every day that closes
with a thankful heart and a mind at peace with those
around us.

Sirach 48:1–4, 9–11
Psalm 80
Matthew 17:9a, 10–13

*As the earth brings forth its plants,*
*and a garden makes its growth spring up,*
*So will the Lord GOD make justice and praise*
*spring up before all the nations.*

—ISAIAH 61:11

God's creation is organic, dynamic, alive, and always growing big dreams from tiny possibilities. Just as God draws the fruit and the flower from a little seed, so, too, God is drawing the very best from every person and every nation.

Isaiah 61:1–2, 10–11
Luke 1:46–50, 53–54
1 Thessalonians 5:16–24
John 1:6–8, 19–28

*[The angel] said, "Hail, full of grace! The Lord is with you." But
she was greatly troubled at what was said and pondered what sort of
greeting this might be. Then the angel said to her, "Do not be afraid,
Mary, for you have found favor with God. Behold, you will conceive
in your womb and bear a son, and you shall name him Jesus."*

—LUKE 1:28–31

Whenever God's power touches human lives, whether
in dramatic visions or subtle inner movements, our
natural reaction is to feel disturbed and fearful. If we
dare to trust the angel's reassurance, however, our fear
can be transformed into awe and our resistance into
life-changing response.

Zechariah 2:14–17 or Revelation 11:19; 12:1–6, 10
Judith 13:18–19
Luke 1:26–38 or 1:39–47

*On that day*
*You need not be ashamed*
*of all your deeds,*
*your rebellious actions against me;*
*For then will I remove from your midst*
*the proud braggarts,*
*And you shall no longer exalt yourself*
*on my holy mountain.*
—ZEPHANIAH 3:11

Imagine a children's game in which the Barbie dolls and toy soldiers come alive and take over the planet. I sometimes wonder whether this is how we appear to God as we strut around on God's holy mountain, Earth.

Zephaniah 3:1–2, 9–13
Psalm 34
Matthew 21:28–32

*I am the LORD, there is no other;*
*I form the light, and create the darkness,*
*I make well-being and create woe;*
*I, the LORD, do all these things.*

—ISAIAH 45:6

We could read this comment as an expression of the illusion we have of being the center of the universe. It is the task of a lifetime to recognize this as the illusion it is and then to discover that God alone is the axis around which all creation spins.

Isaiah 45:6–8, 18, 21–25
Psalm 85
Luke 7:18–23

*Though the mountains leave their place*
*and the hills be shaken,*
*My love shall never leave you*
*nor my covenant of peace be shaken.*
—ISAIAH 54:10

In the devastation left behind by the most disastrous earthquake, we find human hands reaching out to feed the starving and bind the wounded. In the wake of a catastrophic tsunami, we hear the march of human feet rushing to help and to rescue. These are the hands and feet of Christ.

Will ours be among them?

Isaiah 54:1–10
Psalm 30
Luke 7:24–30

*Thus says the LORD:*
*Observe what is right, do what is just;*
*for my salvation is about to come,*
*my justice, about to be revealed.*

—ISAIAH 56:1

There is a causal connection here. It is those who care for justice and act with integrity who are preparing the way for the salvation we long for. And it is those whose hearts are just and whose eyes see the truth who will recognize it when it is revealed.

Isaiah 56:1–3, 6–8
Psalm 67
John 5:33–36

*The mountains shall yield peace for the people,*
*and the hills justice.*

—PSALM 72:3

All creation is striving to bring forth a mystery beyond itself, a kingdom of peace and justice. The created world models it, the prophets foretell it, the psalmist celebrates it, and Jesus shows us what it looks like in reality. All of these invite us to let God's kingdom come to birth in our own lives.

Genesis 49:2, 8–10
Psalm 72
Matthew 1:1–17

*The angel said to her in reply, "The Holy Spirit will come upon you,*
*and the power of the Most High will overshadow you."*

—LUKE 1:35

The mere shadow of God is brighter than our brightest
sunlight, and it rests upon us with a generative, life-giving
power that bursts open our imagination and potential.

2 Samuel 7:1–5, 8–12, 14, 16
Psalm 89
Romans 16:25–27
Luke 1:26–38

*But now you will be speechless and unable to talk until the day these things take place, because you did not believe my words, which will be fulfilled at their proper time.*

—LUKE 1:20

I pray that if I do not speak from a baseline of faith and trust, I, too, might be silenced, or at the very least that others might have the good sense not to listen to me.

Judges 13:2–7, 24–25
Psalm 71
Luke 1:5–25

# DECEMBER 20

*He shall receive a blessing from the LORD,*
*a reward from God his savior.*
*Such is the race that seeks for him,*
*that seeks the face of the God of Jacob.*

—PSALM 24: 5–6

Do we dare offer God the blank check of our hearts and souls and lives? Can we do this—will we do it—knowing that it may cost us all we have and all we are?

Isaiah 7:10–14
Psalm 24
Luke 1:26–38

*Blessed are you who believed that what was spoken to you by the Lord would be fulfilled.*

—LUKE 1:45

God's promises are like seeds. If they take root in our hearts, if we really trust them, then they will grow to fulfillment and bear the fruits of blessing for ourselves and for others.

Song of Songs 2:8–14 or Zephaniah 3:14–18
Psalm 33
Luke 1:39–45

*I prayed for this child, and the LORD granted my request. Now I, in turn, give him to the LORD; as long as he lives, he shall be dedicated to the LORD.*

—1 SAMUEL 1:27–28

When a gift we have longed for and that truly comes from God is actually given to us, then a strange thing happens. We lose any desire to keep it all to ourselves and experience instead a desire to give it back to God, to be multiplied and shared among many.

1 Samuel 1:24–28
1 Samuel 2:1, 4–8
Luke 1:46–56

*All who heard these things took them to heart, saying, "What, then, will this child be?" For surely the hand of the Lord was with him.*

—LUKE 1:66

Whenever we gaze at a newborn baby we might ask, "What fragment of God's dream will this new life reveal?" The newborn John was to become the pointer to the One who would reveal all of it.

Malachi 3:1–4, 23–24
Psalm 25
Luke 1:57–66

*You, my child, shall be called prophet of the Most High,*
*for you will go before the Lord to prepare his way,*
*to give his people knowledge of salvation*
*by the forgiveness of their sins.*

—LUKE 1: 76–77

We stand, tonight, on the threshold of the new covenant.
Leadership now rests in the hands of a little child who
comes, helpless, humble, and poor, to prepare human
hearts and minds for a new vision of God's dream for
God's people. This little child will turn all our assumptions
on their heads. Will we recognize him? Will we have the
courage to follow where he leads?

2 Samuel 7:1–5, 8–12, 14, 16
Psalm 89
Luke 1:67–79

*Sunday*

# DECEMBER 25

• THE NATIVITY OF THE LORD • CHRISTMAS •

> *What came to be through him was life,*
> *and this life was the light of the human race;*
> *the light shines in the darkness,*
> *and the darkness has not overcome it.*
>
> —JOHN 1:3–5

A first-century philosopher observed: "When I light a candle at midnight, I say to the darkness: 'I beg to differ.'" As we light our Christmas candles, we, too, say to the darkness in our world and in our own hearts, "You have no final power over us, for the first and final word is eternal light."

| Vigil: | Dawn: |
|---|---|
| Isaiah 62:1–5 | Isaiah 62:11–12 |
| Psalm 89 | Psalm 97 |
| Acts 13:16–17, 22–25 | Titus 3:4–7 |
| Matthew 1:1–25 or 1:18–25 | Luke 2:15–20 |
| **Midnight:** | **Day:** |
| Isaiah 9:1–6 | Isaiah 52:7–10 |
| Psalm 96 | Psalm 98 |
| Titus 2:11–14 | Hebrews 1:1–6 |
| Luke 2:1–14 | John 1:1–18 or 1:1–5, 9–14 |

*But he, filled with the Holy Spirit, looked up intently to heaven and saw the glory of God and Jesus standing at the right hand of God, and he said, "Behold, I see the heavens opened and the Son of Man standing at the right hand of God."*

—ACTS 7:55–56

The stones that battered Stephen's body broke open the doorways of his soul to reveal to him the eternal promise of God, transcending the very worst that human cruelty can inflict.

Acts 6:8–10, 7:54–59
Psalm 31
Matthew 10:17–22

*For the life was made visible;*
*we have seen it and testify to it*
*and proclaim to you the eternal life*
*that was with the Father and was made visible to us.*

—1 JOHN 1:2

A little girl discovered her granny spinning golden thread in the midst of a dark and dangerous forest. As a token of her love, Granny tied one end of the thread to the child's finger and sent her back to the forest with the promise: "Wherever you go, whatever happens, you are connected to me by this golden thread, which can never be broken." Jesus is to us the visible evidence of God's continuous presence and love.

1 John 1:1–4
Psalm 97
John 20:1a, 2–8

*This is the message that we have heard from Jesus Christ and proclaim
to you: God is light, and in him there is no darkness at all. If we say,
"We have fellowship with him," while we continue to walk in darkness,
we lie and do not act in truth.*

—1 JOHN 1:5–6

It takes only one candle to banish the darkness from the
darkest of rooms. It takes only one gleam of faith to banish
the fear from the darkest of situations.

It may be asked of each and any of us, at any time, to light
that single candle in our own situations. In the midst of the
pain, fright, or confusion, we may be the only ones who
have a candle or the faith to light it.

1 John 1:5—2:2
Psalm 124
Matthew 2:13–18

---

*Simeon blessed them and said to Mary his mother, "Behold, this child is destined for the fall and rise of many in Israel, and to be a sign that will be contradicted (and you yourself a sword will pierce) so that the thoughts of many hearts may be revealed."*

—LUKE 2:34–35

I love to think of Jesus having godparents. Today we meet Simeon, whom I like to think of as a godfather to this very special child. His insight penetrates the mystery that he's witnessing. He sees both falling and rising, death and new birth, something wonderfully offered and incredibly rejected. He sees a blade of truth and integrity that will both wound and heal.

1 John 2:3–11
Psalm 96
Luke 2:22–35

⋑ 33 ⋐

*When they had fulfilled all the prescriptions of the law of the Lord, they returned to Galilee, to their own town of Nazareth. The child grew and became strong, filled with wisdom; and the favor of God was upon him.*

—LUKE 2:39–40

The pattern set by the Holy Family holds good for all families in every culture and every age. First, discipline provides the foundation for healthy growth, and growth allows wisdom to emerge, and God's blessing and favor embraces the whole process.

Sirach 3:2–7, 12–14 or Colossians 3:12–21 or 3:12–17
Psalm 128
Luke 2:22–40 or 2:22, 39–40

*He came to what was his own,*
*but his own people did not accept him.*

*But to those who did accept him he gave power to become*
*children of God.*

—JOHN 1:11–12

Tonight in Scotland, the old tradition of first footing will
be reenacted. Will the first person to cross the threshold
of our home in the new year bring blessing? Suppose the
first footer is the One who gives us abundant life. Suppose
God comes asking us to enter God's own domain deep in
our heart. Will we welcome God home, and rejoice in his
promise to lead us into 2012 as his own, his beloved ones?

1 John 2:18–21
Psalm 96
John 1:1–18

*The LORD bless you and keep you!*
*The LORD let his face shine upon you, and be gracious to you!*
*The LORD look upon you kindly and give you peace!*

—NUMBERS 6:24–27

The Lord has blessed me today. A kindly salesperson
pointed out a saving I could make on my purchase.
A trusting blackbird hopped across my path to say,
"Good morning!" My baby granddaughter said,
"I love you, Grandma!" In all of these things, the Lord
uncovered his face to me today, shone his light into my
life, and gave me peace.

Numbers 6:22–27
Psalm 67
Galatians 4:4–7
Luke 2:16–21

• ST. BASIL THE GREAT AND ST. GREGORY NAZIANZEN,
BISHOPS AND DOCTORS OF THE CHURCH •

*Let what you heard from the beginning remain in you.*
*If what you heard from the beginning remains in you,*
*then you will remain in the Son and in the Father.*

—1 JOHN 2:24

What was it that first drew your heart more consciously
toward God? Perhaps a glimpse of the mystery—
something you did not understand but intuited in a
moment of deep peace—or of profound relationship with
another person, or of awe and wonder in some aspect of
God's creation. In such moments, a spring of grace breaks
into our lives and potentially changes everything.
Keep those moments alive. Let them remain alive in
you and continue to empower and assure you.

1 John 2:22–28
Psalm 98
John 1:19–28

# JANUARY 3

*"'A man is coming after me who ranks ahead of me because he existed before me.' I did not know him, but the reason why I came baptizing with water was that he might be made known to Israel."*

—JOHN 1:30–31

John's powerful testimony to the One coming after him is all the more compelling because he didn't yet *know* the man to whom he was bearing witness. Even though John was a prophet, he, too, had to do everything on faith.

1 John 2:29–3:6
Psalm 98
John 1:29–34

# JANUARY 4

• ST. ELIZABETH ANN SETON, RELIGIOUS •

*John was standing with two of his disciples,*
*and as he watched Jesus walk by,*
*he said, "Behold, the Lamb of God."*

—JOHN 1:35

A genuine disciple is one who points beyond him- or herself toward the One who truly is to be followed.

1 John 3:7–10
Psalm 98
John 1:35–42

*Children, let us love not in word or speech but in deed and truth.*

—1 JOHN 3:18

Carl phoned home when his mother fell ill. "I love you, Mom," he assured her. His brother Chris didn't think about phoning. He got in the car and turned up at the door. "I came right over, Mom," he said. "What can I do?"

1 John 3:11–21
Psalm 100
John 1:43–51

# JANUARY 6

*One mightier than I is coming after me. I am not worthy to stoop
and loosen the thongs of his sandals.*

—MARK 1:7

In our cutthroat society, we take it for granted that those
who are up front are the ones who have the power and
the glory. The gospel turns that attitude on its head. John
knows that the One who comes behind him is the One
who truly leads and that the feet that humbly follow walk
in sandals he is unworthy to loosen.

1 John 5:5–13
Psalm 147
Mark 1:7–11 or Luke 3:23–38 or Luke 3:23, 31–34, 36, 38

*Everyone serves good wine first, and then when people have drunk freely, an inferior one; but you have kept the good wine until now.*

—JOHN 2:10

"I want it now!" That could be the slogan of our consumer society. Yet God prefers to wait for the wine of our souls to mature gradually, and only then does God reveal the full flavor of the feast.

1 John 5:14–21
Psalm 149
John 2:1–11

*They were overjoyed at seeing the star, and on entering the house they saw the child with Mary his mother. They prostrated themselves and did him homage. Then they opened their treasures and offered him gifts of gold, frankincense, and myrrh.*

—MATTHEW 2:10–11

First the strange visitors were overjoyed, and then they offered their gifts. True gifts of love always work this way. First we are filled with the love that God freely pours into our hearts, and only then can we pass on that gift to others and back to God, from whom all gifting comes.

Isaiah 60:1–6
Psalm 72
Ephesians 3:2–3, 5–6
Matthew 2:1–12

*On coming up out of the water he saw the heavens being torn open and
the Spirit, like a dove, descending upon him. And a voice came from the
heavens, "You are my beloved Son; with you I am well pleased."*

—MARK 1:10–11

A friend of mine, a songwriter, has composed a lovely song
about Jesus' baptism. He uses these words to express God's
favor resting upon Jesus: "You are everything I knew you
could become." Just imagine, when we stand face to face
with our Creator, will we also hear such words: "You are
everything I knew you could become."

Isaiah 42:1–4, 6–7, or Isaiah 55:1–11
Psalm 29
Acts 10:34–38 or 1 John 5:1–9
Mark 1:7–11

# JANUARY 10

*What is this? A new teaching with authority.*
*He commands even the unclean spirits and they obey him.*
—MARK 1:27

Our hearts recognize authentic teaching. It is rare and
unexpected, and it resonates with startling clarity and
simplicity. It speaks from timeless wisdom. What is false
within us flees before such teaching, and all that is true
responds and follows it.

1 Samuel 1:9–20
1 Samuel 2:1, 4–5, 6–8
Mark 1:21–28
Or
1 Samuel 1:1–8, 9–20
Mark 1:14–20, 21–28

*Let us go on to the neaby villages that I may preach there also.*
*For this purpose have I come.*

—MARK 1:38

Because we have good news to share, let us also be willing
to go to where the people are, even though that takes us
where we may feel strange, unwelcome, and uncomfortable.

1 Samuel 3:1–10, 19–20
Psalm 40
Mark 1:29–39

⇒ 46 ⇐

*The man went away and began to publicize the whole matter.*
*He spread the report abroad so that it was impossible for Jesus to*
*enter a town openly. He remained outside in deserted places,*
*and people kept coming to him from everywhere.*

—MARK 1:45

Jesus surely holds especially dear those of his friends who
dare follow him to the dark and lonely "outside" places of
our world—the ghettos, the prisons, the homeless shelters,
the threatening city streets—and bring God's love and
truth to those they find there.

1 Samuel 4:1–11
Psalm 44
Mark 1:40–45

[Jesus] said to the paralytic, "I say to you, rise, pick up your mat, and go home." He rose, picked up his mat at once, and went away in the sight of everyone.

—MARK 2:11–12

In the presence and power of Jesus, the fears and limitations that paralyze us are superseded by his irresistible call to go beyond them. Will we have the courage, like the paralytic, to get up and walk?

1 Samuel 8:4–7, 10–22
Psalm 89
Mark 2:1–12

*Why does he eat with tax collectors and sinners?*
—MARK 2:16

I wonder how this question would sound in our twenty-first-century world.

"Why does he hang out with dropouts?"

"Why does he befriend illegals?"

"Why is he so often down at the wrong end of town?"

"Why does he go out of his way to be with those we go out of our way to avoid?"

1 Samuel 9:1–4, 17–19; 10:1
Psalm 21
Mark 2:13–17

# JANUARY 15

*Then Eli understood that the LORD was calling the youth.*
*So he said to Samuel, "Go to sleep, and if you are called, reply,*
*'Speak, LORD, for your servant is listening.'"*

—1 SAMUEL 3:8–9

Eli understands the secret of discernment,
of discovering God's will:

Be still.

Listen for the stirring of God in your soul.

And then, respond.

1 Samuel 3:3–10, 19
Psalm 40
1 Corinthians 6:13–15, 17–20
John 1:35–42

*No one sews a piece of unshrunken cloth on an old cloak. If he does, its fullness pulls away, the new from the old, and the tear gets worse.*

—MARK 2:21

God doesn't apply Band-Aids to our wounded lives and wounded world. God renews and restores us to wholeness, into a seamless, unpatched garment of love.

1 Samuel 15:16–23
Psalm 50
Mark 2:18–22

# JANUARY 17

• ST. ANTHONY, ABBOT •

*The sabbath was made for man, not man for the sabbath.*
*That is why the Son of Man is lord even of the sabbath.*
—MARK 2:27–28

I once had the joy of attending a concert given by the Soweto Gospel Choir. The effect of the music was electric, and everyone was literally dancing in the aisles. The utter freedom was palpable, yet that freedom and fullness of expression was absolutely interwoven with a powerful collective discipline that kept them practicing and acutely aware of their own exact notes and rhythms in the glorious music of the whole performance.

Freedom flows best within the framework of discipline. And discipline is meaningful only if it enables authentic freedom.

1 Samuel 16:1–13
Psalm 89
Mark 2:23–28

# JANUARY 18

*Thus David overcame the Philistine with sling and stone;*
*he struck the Philistine mortally, and did it without a sword.*

—1 SAMUEL 17:50

The most effective agents for peace and justice in our
world have been those such as Mahatma Gandhi or
Martin Luther King Jr., and of course Jesus himself,
who confronted the might of overwhelming domination
with just the sling and stone of truth and integrity.

1 Samuel 17:32–33, 37, 40–51
Psalm 144
Mark 3:1–6

# JANUARY 19

*My wanderings you have counted;*
*my tears are stored in your flask;*
*are they not recorded in your book?*
—PSALM 56:9

Carol and Carl, in their later years, would often reminisce about incidents in the childhood years of their kids. They would smile over every adventure each child had embarked on, and the ways in which each had worked out his or her own pathway through life. And they never forgot the distress calls in the night or the tearful times of loss and disappointment that each child had known through the years. Everything was imprinted forever on the canvas of their own lives. In their own family, they were reflections of God's unceasing knowledge of us, God's children.

1 Samuel 18:6–9; 19:1–7
Psalm 56
Mark 3:7–12

*Saul then said to David: "You are in the right rather than I;*
*you have treated me generously, while I have done you harm."*

—1 SAMUEL 24:18

Tina's new colleagues gave her a hard time. One in
particular never missed an opportunity for a spiteful
put-down. At first Tina's instinct was to respond in
anger. Gradually, she started to withdraw into herself,
her confidence shaken. Finally, she hit upon the idea
of repaying evil with good: she baked a cake for her
colleagues and invited them to a little office party. She had
moved beyond her inner Saul to her inner David, and her
colleagues, surprised by kindness, slowly began to change
their attitude.

1 Samuel 24:3–21
Psalm 57
Mark 3:13–19

*Jesus came with his disciples into the house. Again the crowd gathered, making it impossible for them even to eat. When his relatives heard of this they set out to seize him, for they said, "He is out of his mind."*

—MARK 3:20–21

Sometimes we have to get "out of our mind" before
we can really connect with our heart. This may cause
consternation in those around us and in ourselves, but it is
the way of Jesus and is the paradoxical logic of God.

2 Samuel 1:1–4, 11–12, 19, 23–27
Psalm 80
Mark 3:20–21

*[Jesus said,] "This is the time of fulfillment. The kingdom of God is at hand. Repent, and believe in the gospel."*

—MARK 1:15

The time for turning in a new direction often comes when, like a bucket in a well, we reach rock bottom. With our own resources exhausted, we have to throw ourselves onto the mercy of God. At such a point all we can do is trust, and let our turning become a re-turning to the One who has never left us.

Jonah 3:1–5, 10
Psalm 25
1 Corinthians 7:29–31
Mark 1:14–20

*The scribes who had come from Jerusalem said of Jesus, "He is possessed by Beelzebul," and "By the prince of demons he drives out demons."*

—MARK 3:22–23

The effect of evil is to multiply our confusion and confound our reason. The effect of God's goodness is to bring peace, calm, and clarity. Evil can never overcome evil but only magnify it. Only goodness can overcome evil and transform it into good.

2 Samuel 5:1–7, 10
Psalm 89
Mark 3:22–30

*But [Jesus] said to them in reply, "Who are my mother and my brothers?" And looking around at those seated in the circle he said, "Here are my mother and my brothers. For whoever does the will of God is my brother and sister and mother."*

—MARK 3:33–35

The whole human family is my family. Each person is my brother or my sister. I wonder how long it will be before our sibling rivalries change and grow up to be brotherly and sisterly love.

2 Samuel 6:12–15, 17–19
Psalm 24
Mark 3:31–35

*"Saul, my brother, the Lord has sent me, Jesus who appeared to you on the way by which you came, that you may regain your sight and be filled with the Holy Spirit." Immediately things like scales fell from his eyes and he regained his sight.*

—ACTS 9:17–18

Sometimes it is the person we least expect who comes in sideways to a situation and opens our eyes to a very different point of view. Has this ever happened to you?

Acts 22:3–16 or Acts 9:1–22
Psalm 117
Mark 16:15–18

# JANUARY 26

• ST. TIMOTHY AND ST. TITUS, BISHOPS •

*I am grateful to God, whom I worship with a clear conscience*
*as my ancestors did, as I remember you constantly in my prayers,*
*night and day.*

—2 TIMOTHY 1:3

There are three gifts of grace:

gratitude,

the faithful performance of duty,

and prayer.

2 Timothy 1:1–8 or Titus 1:1–5
Psalm 132
Mark 4:21–25

*[Jesus] said, "To what shall we compare the Kingdom of God, or what parable can we use for it? It is like a mustard seed that, when it is sown in the ground, is the smallest of all the seeds on the earth. But once it is sown, it springs up and becomes the largest of plants and puts forth large branches, so that the birds of the sky can dwell in its shade."*

—MARK 4:30–32

"The best things come in small packages," the saying goes. It shouldn't surprise us, therefore, that God's kingdom comes in the smallest possible form: a tiny seed planted in an open, receptive heart. Then it grows and grows until it becomes the place where many who are lost and lonely find a home.

2 Samuel 11:1–10, 13–17
Psalm 51
Mark 4:26–34

# JANUARY 28

• ST. THOMAS AQUINAS, PRIEST AND DOCTOR OF THE CHURCH •

*Leaving the crowd, they took Jesus with them in the boat just as he was.*
*And other boats were with him. A violent squall came up and waves*
*were breaking over the boat, so that it was already filling up.*
*Jesus was in the stern, asleep on a cushion.*

—MARK 4:36–38

Who among us has never experienced these storms—
within and around us—felt the gales of opposition blowing,
known the waves of despair or helplessness that swamp us.
But when these storms arise, do we think of waking up the
Lord, who is the unchangeable presence of peace in the
eye of the storm?

2 Samuel 12:1–7, 10–17
Psalm 51
Mark 4:35–41

# JANUARY 29

*A prophet like me will the LORD, your God, raise up for you from among your own kin; to him you shall listen.*

—DEUTERONOMY 18:15

God continues to raise up prophets in our own times, from among ourselves. Where do we hear these prophetic voices among us today, and do we listen to them and act on their wisdom?

Deuteronomy 18:15–20
Psalm 95
1 Corinthians 7:32–35
Mark 1:21–28

*"What have you to do with me, Jesus, Son of the Most High God? I adjure you by God, do not torment me!" (He had been saying to him, "Unclean spirit, come out of the man!") He asked him, "What is your name?" He replied, "Legion is my name. There are many of us."*

—MARK 5:7–9

Sometimes I think that when a good thought or intention comes to mind, a dozen demons follow in its wake, trying to strangle it out of existence: "It'll never work"; "You're too busy right now"; "You'll make a fool of yourself if you say that." There's no need to name all of those demons, for there are so many of them. But over all their insistent clamor, the clear tones of God come through: "Come out of her, negative spirits, and leave her free to do what I am asking."

2 Samuel 15:13–14, 30; 16:5–13
Psalm 3
Mark 5:1–20

# JANUARY 31

*That day's victory was turned into mourning for the whole army when
they heard that the king was grieving for his son.*

—2 SAMUEL 19:3

On the television news, a clip shows a young soldier in
Afghanistan cradling an injured child, tears welling up in
his eyes. When the delicate light of human compassion and
sorrow flickers across our fields of conflict, military victory
seems but a hollow gain.

2 Samuel 18:9–10, 14, 24–25, 30; 19:3
Psalm 86
Mark 5:21–43

*For this shall every faithful man pray to you*
*in time of stress.*
*Though deep waters overflow,*
*they shall not reach him.*
—PSALM 32:6

It is a rare human being who doesn't occasionally feel
inundated by circumstances or flooded with anxiety or
fear. My own coping mechanism in these moments is to
withdraw, if even for a short time, to a quiet space and
focus my mind and heart on the God who is above and
beyond all the stress. When I do that, I discover that the
psalmist is right: the floods may rise high, but they will
never totally submerge me.

2 Samuel 24:2, 9–17
Psalm 32
Mark 6:1–6

*He will sit refining and purifying silver,*
*and he will purify the sons of Levi,*
*Refining them like gold or like silver*
*that they may offer due sacrifice to the LORD.*

—MALACHI 3:3

A silversmith was once asked, "How can you tell when the silver has been long enough in the refining fire?" He replied, "When I can see my own image reflected in it."

By today's candlelight let us gaze with Simeon and Anna on the image of God in its perfection, the infant Jesus.

Malachi 3:1–4
Psalm 24
Hebrews 2:14–18
Luke 2:22–40 or Luke 2:22–32

*Friday*

# FEBRUARY 3

*With his every deed he offered thanks
to God Most High, in words of praise.
With his whole being he loved his Maker
and daily had his praises sung.*
—SIRACH 47:8

It's always obvious when something is being offered from the
heart or merely from the head. What is offered from the head
may be full of good information; we will listen attentively,
learn something from it, and maybe take notes. But what
is offered from the heart—whether a song or a prayer or a
meal—has a life of its own. The offering brings those who
receive it to a deeper and more vibrant life themselves.

Sirach 47:2–11
Psalm 18
Mark 6:14–29

# FEBRUARY 4

*When Jesus disembarked and saw the vast crowd, his heart was moved*
*with pity for them, for they were like sheep without a shepherd;*
*and he began to teach them many things.*

—MARK 6:34

On a walk on a Welsh hillside, I found that I was being
followed! A flock of hopeful sheep trailed after me across
the field, and I thought that the farmer probably brought
them food at that hour of the afternoon. Sheep will go
where they think the food is. No wonder so many hungry
hearts flocked after Jesus. The Good Shepherd not only
guides and protects his sheep; he also feeds the flock.
How, and where, does he feed you?

1 Kings 3:4–13
Psalm 119
Mark 6:30–34

# FEBRUARY 5

*Simon's mother-in-law lay sick with a fever. They immediately told him*
*about her. He approached, grasped her hand, and helped her up.*
*Then the fever left her and she waited on them.*

—MARK 1:30–31

Simon's mother-in-law could be the patron saint of twenty-
first century western society—the patron saint of fevered
lives and activity. Can we learn from this incident? Can we
learn to bring the fever to God, who alone can calm and
cool it? Can we put our own hands into the hand of God
and let God help us up? Can we let the process change
our focus, away from the things that cause the fever and
toward the ways in which we might better serve one
another?

Job 7:1–4, 6–7
Psalm 147
1 Corinthians 9:16–19, 22–23
Mark 1:29–39

*The LORD intends to dwell in the dark cloud.*

—1 KINGS 8:12

And don't we know it! God, the impenetrable mystery.
God, the stirring in our hearts that we can't define or
name. God, the elusive ground of our being, the presence
that calls us continually beyond our own horizons.
May we have the grace to trust the dark cloud,
for it is the very dwelling place of God.

1 Kings 8:1–7, 9–13
Psalm 132
Mark 6:53–56

*Can it indeed be that God dwells on earth? If the heavens and the highest heavens cannot contain you, how much less this temple which I have built!*

—1 KINGS 8:27

However magnificent the houses we build for God may be, God will never be contained by them. However well thought out our mental categories for understanding the divine may be, the divine will always flow out of and beyond the boxes. If we could contain the mystery, the mystery would not be God.

1 Kings 8:22–23, 27–30
Psalm 84
Mark 7:1–13

*Nothing that enters one from outside can defile that person;*
*but the things that come out from within are what defile.*

—MARK 7:15

Although nothing outside us can make us "unclean" inside,
the ugliness around us can activate and aggravate the
ugliness in our hearts. It's also true that beauty around us
draws forth the beauty within us. How very important it
becomes, therefore, to strive to make the world a more
beautiful place that truly reflects the image of God
deep in our hearts.

1 Kings 10:1–10
Psalm 37
Mark 7:14–23

*They served their idols,*
*which became a snare for them.*
—PSALM 106:36

Perhaps today's most potent idol is money. Our worship of this idol has ensnared us, it has led us into all the addictions of a consumer mind-set, from which it has become almost impossible to extricate ourselves or our children.

1 Kings 11:4–13
Psalm 106
Mark 7:24–30

*"He has done all things well.*
*He makes the deaf hear and the mute speak."*
—MARK 7:37

Springtime returns after a long, hard winter. All around,
new life burgeons, in bud and blossom, bird and beast.
The sounds of springtime penetrate even the deafest
of ears, closed down by winter's fog, and call forth
spontaneous rejoicing from lips that have long been sealed
against the winter cold. God is calling to our hearts anew,
and our joy echoes back across the green valley.

Take a moment to remember seasons of springtime in
your own heart's journey, and give thanks for them.

1 Kings 11:29–32; 12:19
Psalm 81
Mark 7:31–37

# FEBRUARY 11

*They made a calf in Horeb*
*and adored a molten image;*
*They exchanged their glory*
*for the image of a grass-eating bullock.*

—PSALM 106:19–20

A mountain invites us to look up to everything that we can
become and to follow that vision. But if we so choose, it
allows us to settle down in our comfort zone, leaving the
ascent to others and contenting ourselves with far less than
we really long for. Life is a mountain. How will we focus
our gaze: up or down?

1 Kings 12:26–32; 13:33–34
Psalm 106
Mark 8:1–10

# FEBRUARY 12

*Brothers and sisters, whether you eat or drink, or whatever you do,
do everything for the glory of God.*

—1 CORINTHIANS 10:31

I spend—or rather waste—a lot of time agonizing about
all the good things I haven't done and probably will never
do. Indeed, I reproach myself for not doing things I am
probably not even gifted to do. This drains me of the
energy I need to do those one or two things that
I *can* do and to do them to the very best of my ability. God
doesn't ask us to travel every possible path through life.
God asks us to walk just one path—our own path—and to
walk it with integrity and passion.

Leviticus 13:1–2, 44–46
Psalm 32
1 Corinthians 10:31–11:1
Mark 1:40–45

*For the sun comes up with its scorching heat and dries up the grass, its flower droops, and the beauty of its appearance vanishes. So will the rich person fade away in the midst of his pursuits.*

—JAMES 1:11

Riches can disappear even faster than the sun can rise: the click of a mouse in the stock exchange or the sleight of hand that clones our credit card. May God give us the wisdom not to build our lives on a shifting sandbar.

James 1:1–11
Psalm 119
Mark 8:11–13

# FEBRUARY 14

*When I say, "My foot is slipping,"*
*your mercy, O LORD, sustains me;*
*When cares abound within me,*
*your comfort gladdens my soul.*
—PSALM 94:18–19

From losing to holding, from cares to calm—the peace of
God grips us when we lose grip on ourselves.

The calm of God draws us to depths below our turbulence.

Spend a moment with the psalmist today and see what he
has to say to you.

James 1:12–18
Psalm 94
Mark 8:14–21

# FEBRUARY 15

*He who walks blamelessly and does justice;*
*who thinks the truth in his heart*
*and slanders not with his tongue.*

—PSALM 15:2–35

Have I learned not to make promises that I may not be able
to keep and to keep those promises that I do make?
Have I learned to give of myself, my time, and my gifts
without expecting any reward?
Have I learned to do what is right just because it is right
and not because it might bring me profit?
Hard lessons! And we are learning all of them in the
foothills of the holy mountain.

James 1:19–27
Psalm 15
Mark 8:22–26

# FEBRUARY 16

*Listen, my beloved brothers and sisters. Did not God choose those who are poor in the world to be rich in faith and heirs of the Kingdom that he promised to those who love him?*

—JAMES 2:5

Only those hands that are empty and open can receive all that God is longing to give.

Hands that are full of themselves, of their own achievements and successes, will have no room for the "more" that the kingdom will reveal.

James 2:1–9
Psalm 34
Mark 8:27–33

*So also faith of itself, if it does not have works, is dead.*

—JAMES 2:17

To imagine that faith is something we can learn from
books and lectures, or even from creeds and catechisms,
is like imagining that we can learn to swim without getting
into the water. Faith in a God of justice and compassion
is meaningful only if it makes us more just and more
compassionate in everything we do.

James 2:14–24, 26
Psalm 112
Mark 8:34–9:1

*Consider how small a fire can set a huge forest ablaze.*
*The tongue is also a fire.*

—JAMES 3:5–6

A story tells of a woman who was given to malicious gossip. One day a wise mentor told her to take her feather pillow to the top of her house, open a window, and shake it out, scattering the feathers to the four winds. No problem! But then came the difficult bit: "Now go out and collect all the feathers again and put them back in the pillow." Impossible! May we never underestimate the power of unkind words to spread like wildfire.

James 3:1–10
Psalm 12
Mark 9:2–13

*They came bringing to him a paralytic carried by four men.
Unable to get near Jesus because of the crowd, they opened up the roof
above him. After they had broken through, they let down the mat on
which the paralytic was lying.*

—MARK 2:3–4

His friends "let down" the paralytic, on a stretcher.
We have all been let down from time to time, by people
or by life itself. This beautiful story reminds us that
sometimes being let down can bring us closer to
Jesus than we could have dared to hope.

Isaiah 43:18–19, 21–22, 24–25
Psalm 41
2 Corinthians 1:18–23
Mark 2:1–12

*Then the boy's father cried out, "I do believe, help my unbelief!"*
—MARK 9:24

Acknowledging that the only faith we can muster is minimal is in itself an act of faith, as well as a truly honest statement from the heart.

God will always receive and respond to that kind of radical honesty by reaching out to help the little faith we have.

James 3:13–18
Psalm 19
Mark 9:14–29

*Where do the wars and where do the conflicts among you come from?*
*Is it not from your passions that make war within your members?*
*You covet but do not possess. You kill and envy but you cannot obtain;*
*you fight and wage war.*

—JAMES 4:1–2

This passage sounds like the history of the human race. But might it also be the story of our own hearts? A shocking thought, but perhaps the only way to understand the path that leads to transformation.

James 4:1–10
Psalm 55
Mark 9:30–37

# FEBRUARY 22

• ASH WEDNESDAY •

*Rend your hearts, not your garments,*
*and return to the LORD, your God.*
*For gracious and merciful is he,*
*slow to anger, rich in kindness,*
*and relenting in punishment.*

—JOEL 2:13

I have a friend who lives with her boisterous young family in an apartment in the city. Her prayer space is a view from her window, a tree that changes constantly through the seasons while remaining firmly rooted. Gazing at her tree brings her heart into focus with God.

Where is that prayer space for you?

Joel 2:12–18
Psalm 51
2 Corinthians 5:20–6:2
Matthew 6:1–6, 16–18

---

# FEBRUARY 23

*For whoever wishes to save his life will lose it, but whoever loses his life for my sake will save it. What profit is there for one to gain the whole world yet lose or forfeit himself?*

—LUKE 9:24–25

Jenny longed to learn to skate, but she was a fearful child. She did not dare let go of the rail at the edge of the ice rink, for fear of falling and getting hurt. She never discovered the joy of the ice-dance.

Every new step forward in the dance of life demands that we let go of our safety and trust the One who is the music and the dance, the one who is the dancer within and beyond us.

Deuteronomy 30:15–20
Psalm 1
Luke 9:22–25

# FEBRUARY 24

*For you are not pleased with sacrifices;*
*should I offer a burnt offering, you would not accept it.*
*My sacrifice, O God, is a contrite spirit;*
*a heart contrite and humbled, O God, you will not spurn.*

—PSALM 51:18–19

To sacrifice means, literally, to make something holy or sacred. God doesn't want to sanctify our sackcloth and ashes. God wants to sanctify *us*.

This begins to become possible when we bring ourselves, our hearts, our fears, and our failures into God's presence, just as they are, and beg for the blessing that will never be withheld.

Isaiah 58:1–9
Psalm 51
Matthew 9:14–15

⊰ 90 ⊱

# FEBRUARY 25

*If you remove from your midst oppression,*
*false accusation and malicious speech;*
*If you bestow your bread on the hungry*
*and satisfy the afflicted;*
*Then light shall rise for you in the darkness,*
*and the gloom shall become for you like midday.*

—ISAIAH 58:9–10

We can't give anything to anyone if our fists are clenched.
Giving requires that we open our hands and our hearts
to reach out to others, just as a light source pours out its
light, without restraint, to illuminate all that surrounds it.

Isaiah 58:9–14
Psalm 86
Luke 5:27–32

*The Spirit drove Jesus out into the desert, and he remained in the desert*
*for forty days, tempted by Satan. He was among wild beasts,*
*and the angels ministered to him.*

—MARK 1:12–13

The wilderness is a place—physical, emotional, or
spiritual—where we would usually not choose to be and
would avoid if we could. But in today's Gospel passage,
we discover that it was the Spirit who drove Jesus out into
the wilderness. Next time I find myself in a wilderness
situation, may I have the grace to recognize that it might
be the work of the Spirit bringing me to a place
of challenge and new growth.

Genesis 9:8–15
Psalm 25
1 Peter 3:18–22
Mark 1:12–15

*"Lord, when did we see you hungry or thirsty or a stranger or naked or*
*ill or in prison, and not minister to your needs?" He will answer them,*
*"Amen, I say to you, what you did not do for one of these least ones,*
*you did not do for me."*

—MATTHEW 25:44–45

We didn't want to intrude.

We didn't want to get involved.

We were in a rush to get somewhere else.

We needed our own space.

We couldn't see how we could help.

We thought someone else would step in.

We never noticed . . .

There are so many reasons we fail to recognize Christ in
one another's needs.

Leviticus 19:1–2, 11–18
Psalm 19
Matthew 25:31–46

# FEBRUARY 28

*Just as from the heavens*
*the rain and snow come down*
*And do not return there*
*till they have watered the earth,*
*making it fertile and fruitful . . .*
*So shall my word be . . .*
*It shall not return to me void,*
*but shall do my will,*
*achieving the end for which I sent it.*

—ISAIAH 55:10–11

Nothing can block God's free-flowing love: not our disobedience, fearfulness, or deliberate wrongdoing. God's love is eternal—from God's heart to new creation. Nothing can break this sacred cycle of life-in-God and God-in-life.

Isaiah 55:10–11
Psalm 34
Matthew 6:7–15

# FEBRUARY 29

*Have mercy on me, O God, in your goodness;*
*in the greatness of your compassion wipe out my offense.*
*Thoroughly wash me from my guilt;*
*and of my sin cleanse me.*
—PSALM 51:3–4

A spring of fresh water breaks out of the mountainside.
Wherever it flows, it brings new life and dislodges all the
rubble and detritus along its way.

So, too, the river of God's mercy and compassion flows
through our lives, bringing new life every moment and freeing
us more and more from the rubble and detritus of our guilt.

As we pray this psalm, we consciously invite this all-
powerful love and forgiveness to flow through our lives.

Jonah 3:1–10
Psalm 51
Luke 11:29–32

---

*Which one of you would hand his son a stone when he asked for a loaf of bread, or a snake when he asked for a fish? If you then, who are wicked, know how to give good gifts to your children, how much more will your heavenly Father give good things to those who ask him.*

— MATTHEW 7:9–11

When I was a child, my mother used to say that if there was a patch of blue sky among the clouds big enough to make a sailor's shirt, then it would be fine weather. If we can see just a sliver of pure goodness in humanity, we know that goodness is the ultimate reality. Goodness is God, from whom all human goodness flows.

Esther C12, 14–16, 23–25
Psalm 138
Matthew 7:7–12

*Jesus said to his disciples: "I tell you, unless your righteousness
surpasses that of the scribes and Pharisees,
you will not enter into the Kingdom of heaven."*

—MATTHEW 5:20

It takes only one malicious scratch by vandals to reveal
the bare metal just below the glossy finish of a prized new
car. It takes only one careless movement by a lively child
to spoil the finish on our favorite coffee table. Is the outer
layer of our faith just as easily penetrated, or do we have
solid trust in God underneath the smooth exterior of our
religious observance?

Ezekiel 18:21–28
Psalm 130
Matthew 5:20–26

*For if you love those who love you, what recompense will you have?
Do not the tax collectors do the same? And if you greet your brothers
and sisters only, what is unusual about that? Do not the pagans do the
same? So be perfect, just as your heavenly Father is perfect.*

—MATTHEW 5:46–48

An artist friend of mine has a poster on her kitchen wall
that reads: "Art is lovely. But it takes a lot of time and
effort." Love is like that—such a good idea and sometimes
very easy—but often it takes a lot of time and effort and
makes demands of us that take us where we would rather
not go, with people we would rather not know.

Deuteronomy 26:16–19
Psalm 119
Matthew 5:43–48

*O LORD, I am your servant; . . .*
*you have loosed my bonds.*
*To you will I offer sacrifice of thanksgiving,*
*and I will call upon the name of the LORD.*
—PSALM 116:16

I remember, with enormous gratitude, one or two people through whom God has set me free from fears, prejudices, or illusions. Perhaps I can thank God best by living true to that freedom and opening up small ways for God to loosen the bonds of others.

Genesis 22:1–2, 9–13, 15–18
Psalm 116
Romans 8:31–34
Mark 9:2–10

# MARCH 5

*Jesus said to his disciples: "Be merciful, just as your Father is merciful.*

*"Stop judging and you will not be judged. Stop condemning and you will not be condemned. Forgive and you will be forgiven."*
—LUKE 6:36–37

I was angry when I saw a young man bump carelessly against a mother pushing her baby's stroller along the sidewalk. I was ready to confront him until I saw, just in time, that he was blind. If I can see with God's eyes, then my actions might be guided by God's compassion, and my tendency to judge might become an openness to learn.

Daniel 9:4–10
Psalm 79
Luke 6:36–38

*Why do you recite my statutes,*
*and profess my covenant with your mouth,*
*Though you hate discipline*
*and cast my words behind you?*
—PSALM 50:16–17

What might the psalmist ask of us today? How can you go to church on Sunday and then work against the provision of proper health care for the poorest among you? How can you pray for peace and do nothing to dismantle the machinery of war? How can you listen to sermons and recite creeds, yet be deaf to the cries of the poor and the marginalized? How would we react to such a twenty-first-century psalmist? Would we arrest him and lock him up?

Isaiah 1:10, 16–20
Psalm 50
Matthew 23:1–12

*Whoever wishes to be great among you shall be your servant;*
*whoever wishes to be first among you shall be your slave. Just so,*
*the Son of Man did not come to be served but to serve*
*and to give his life as a ransom for many.*

—MATTHEW 20:26–28

Servants offer food and drink to everyone else before they
sit down to eat their own meal. Servants are inconspicuous;
they wear simple, functional clothes and remain in the
background. Servants' prime concern is the good of others,
even if that means sacrificing their own comfort. We know
what *servant* means. Do you see such signs of service in your
own life, in your family, in your church, or in your nation?

Jeremiah 18:18–20
Psalm 31
Matthew 20:17–28

*More tortuous than all else is the human heart,*
*Beyond remedy; who can understand it?*
*I, the LORD, alone probe the mind*
*and test the heart.*

—JEREMIAH 17:9–10

Our capacity for self-deception is limitless. Our
motivations are a tangled web of good and bad, selfless and
selfish. None of us can probe the depths of our own heart,
let alone the hearts and minds of others. Only the loving
beam of God's heart can penetrate such fog.

Jeremiah 17:5–10
Psalm 1
Luke 16:19–31

*When the chief priests and the Pharisees heard his parables, they knew that he was speaking about them. And although they were attempting to arrest him, they feared the crowds, for they regarded him as a prophet.*

—MATTHEW 21:45–46

In the finest chapters of human history—the abolition of slavery, the end of apartheid in South Africa, the fall of communist oppression in Eastern Europe—the voices of the people have carried the day, against the power of their leaders. Where will our voices be heard in the struggle against corrupt authority in our own times?

Genesis 37:3–4, 12–13, 17–28
Psalm 105
Matthew 21:33–43, 45–46

*For as the heavens are high above the earth,*
*so surpassing is his kindness toward those who fear him.*
*As far as the east is from the west,*
*so far has he put our transgressions from us.*
—PSALM 103:11–12

When my daughter was learning to count and discovering that numbers go on forever, she gave up on the concept of infinity. Instead, she flung her arms around me and declared, "Mom, I love you past numbers."
God loves us past numbers, too.

Micah 7:14–15, 18–20
Psalm 103
Luke 15:1–3, 11–32

*You shall not covet your neighbor's house. You shall not covet your neighbor's wife, nor his male or female slave, nor his ox or ass, nor anything else that belongs to him.*

—EXODUS 20:17

The consumer society, especially in the Western world, depends on a great many people buying things they neither really want nor need, with money that they don't really have. It *depends* on our being persuaded that we covet the things we don't possess. How long before we ask ourselves, Why?

Exodus 20:1–17 or Exodus 20:1–3, 7–8, 12–17
Psalm 19
1 Corinthians 1:22–25
John 2:13–25

*Jesus said to the people in the synagogue at Nazareth: "Amen, I say to
you, no prophet is accepted in his own native place."*

—LUKE 4:24

I once met a lovely woman living a truly simple life in the
flatlands of northern Germany. She had left a career in the
agrochemical industry to study and teach the advantages
of natural therapies and a simpler lifestyle. Her skills and
her enthusiasm attracted people from all over the world to
attend her workshops and seminars. It took fifteen years,
she told us, before a single one of her neighbors showed
any interest in her work.

2 Kings 5:1–15
Psalms 42, 43
Luke 4:24–30

*Good and upright is the LORD;*
*thus he shows sinners the way.*
*He guides the humble to justice,*
*he teaches the humble his way.*

—PSALM 25:8–9

I grew up hearing the saying: "Much would have more."
Now I can see how true it is. The much that I have seduces
me into the byways and cul-de-sacs that I think will lead to
more. The humble and the poor, unburdened by "much,"
are less likely to lose their way.

Daniel 3:25, 34–43
Psalm 25
Matthew 18:21–35

*Jesus said to his disciples: "Do not think that I have come to abolish the law or the prophets. I have come not to abolish but to fulfill."*

—MATTHEW 5:17

We all stand on giants' shoulders. Everything and everyone that has gone before us has helped shape us into who we are. Our journey with God will never be about dismissing or disparaging the past. It is about helping move forward on the journey toward a fulfillment of its divine potential.

Deuteronomy 4:1, 5–9
Psalm 147
Matthew 5:17–19

*Every kingdom divided against itself will be laid waste and house will fall against house.*

—LUKE 11:17

We have long understood that to control a group of people, or whole nations of people, we must "divide and conquer" by setting one faction against another. In that way, no one can see clearly what political manipulations are really going on behind the scenes.

It is not so with God: God's kingdom calls for unity, not division, and it is not about power over others but about empowerment to become the people God created us to be.

Jeremiah 7:23–28
Psalm 95
Luke 11:14–23

*An unfamiliar speech I hear:*
*"I relieved his shoulder of the burden;*
*his hands were freed from the basket.*
*In distress you called, and I rescued you."*
—PSALM 81:6–7

Sometimes we reflect back on difficult times and wonder
how we ever found the strength to pull through and to
move on. In those times, we hear a voice we do not know,
and yet one we know better than our own, whispering
words of reassurance and of promise from deep within us.

Hosea 14:2–10
Psalm 81
Mark 12:28–34

# MARCH 17

*Let us know, let us strive to know the LORD;*
*as certain as the dawn is his coming . . .*
*He will come to us like the rain,*
*like spring rain that waters the earth.*

—HOSEA 6:3

God's presence with us is never in question. But our awareness of that presence comes and goes. Perhaps our main task, as pilgrims along the way of Christ, is to work at that awareness and to discipline ourselves to make quality time for God as often as we can—time in which we determine to know the Lord, in prayer, Scripture, and the unfolding events of daily life.

Hosea 6:1–6
Psalm 51
Luke 18:9–14

⇒ 112 ⇐

*For we are his handiwork, created in Christ Jesus for the good works that God has prepared in advance, that we should live in them.*

—EPHESIANS 2:10

When I walk around a gallery, I see many works of art. Some I like, some I dislike, some I think I understand, and some leave me cold. Yet in each case the artist has expressed something utterly unique and special that only he or she fully knows and loves.

When I walk along the street and look into the eyes of the people I meet, may I have the grace to remember that I am walking through God's own art gallery.

2 Chronicles 36:14–16, 19–23
Psalm 137
Ephesians 2:4–10
John 3:14–21

*"Joseph, son of David, do not be afraid to take Mary your wife*
*into your home. For it is through the Holy Spirit that*
*this child has been conceived in her."*

—MATTHEW 1:20

When God begins to move and grow and make a difference
in a person's life, those who are close to that person
can become very fearful. The closer they are, the more
threatened they may feel. May the angel's reassurance to
Joseph re-echo in our hearts, too, and help us trust that
where God is coming to birth, there can be nothing to fear.

2 Samuel 7:4–5, 12–14, 16
Psalm 89
Romans 4:13, 16–18, 22
Matthew 1:16, 18–21, 24, or Luke 2:41–51

*This water flows into the eastern district down upon the Arabah,
and empties into the sea, the salt waters, which it makes fresh.
Wherever the river flows, every sort of living creature that can multiply
shall live, and there shall be abundant fish, for wherever this water
comes the sea shall be made fresh.*

—EZEKIEL 47:8–9

The clear running water of the Spirit flows through our lives,
bringing refreshment, renewal, and a whole new dimension
to ordinary existence. Sometimes it takes human form: a
child's ingenuous comment or spontaneous display of love,
or a moment of truth that shakes us out of complacency, or a
fresh perspective on a situation that has become deadlocked.
All come from God, and wherever such freshness flows, it
brings renewed health and teeming life.

Ezekiel 47:1–9, 12
Psalm 46
John 5:1–16

*Saying to the prisoners: Come out!*
*To those in darkness: Show yourselves!*
*Along the ways they shall find pasture,*
*on every bare height shall their pastures be.*
*They shall not hunger or thirst,*
*nor shall the scorching wind or the sun strike them;*
*For he who pities them leads them*
*and guides them beside springs of water.*

—ISAIAH 49:9–10

What a difference between the images of darkness, captivity, concealment, tension, and coercion, and the images of grazing, free pasture, abundance, calm, and trustworthy guidance. Such is the contrast between our worlds—when we walk alone or we walk with God.

Isaiah 49:8–15
Psalm 145
John 5:17–30

*[John] was a burning and shining lamp, and for a while you were content to rejoice in his light. But I have testimony greater than John's.*

—JOHN 5:35–36

The warm glow of candlelight gives us contentment
and joy, but its power is nothing compared with
the coming of dawn.

Exodus 32:7–14
Psalm 106
John 5:31–47

# MARCH 23

> *The LORD is close to the brokenhearted,*
> *and those who are crushed in spirit he saves.*
> *Many are the troubles of the just man,*
> *but out of them all the LORD delivers him.*
> —PSALM 34:19–20

Martha was old and arthritic, yet she still loved to walk around her garden, stooping every so often to gather up a flower snapped off by the wind, or to revive a thirsty seedling, or to repot a plant that a stray dog had crushed. Martha showed God's love to the least blade of grass. How much more will God extend such love and tenderness to Martha, and to us!

Wisdom 2:1, 12–22
Psalm 34
John 7:1–2, 10, 25–30

*So the guards went to the chief priests and Pharisees, who asked them, "Why did you not bring him?" The guards answered, "Never before has anyone spoken like this man." So the Pharisees answered them, "Have you also been deceived? Have any of the authorities or the Pharisees believed in him? But this crowd, which does not know the law, is accursed."*

—JOHN 7:45–49

Far from being accursed, the untutored crowd (some Bible translations say *rabble*) recognizes God's authentic voice in Jesus' teaching. Even the armed guards dare not confront this unique authority that's so new to their experience, yet resonates with what they know to be true. Often truth reaches the hearts of ordinary people more directly than it does those who think they have all the answers.

Jeremiah 11:18–20
Psalm 7
John 7:40–53

---

*Unless a grain of wheat falls to the ground and dies, it remains just a grain of wheat; but if it dies, it produces much fruit.*

—JOHN 12:24

We hear these words of Jesus and nod our heads in agreement. Why are we so reluctant to live by them— to let things in our lives die when their time has come, and trust in the promise of the grain of wheat?

Jeremiah 31:31–34
Psalm 51
Hebrews 5:7–9
John 12:20–33

*Therefore the Lord himself will give you this sign: the virgin shall be with child, and bear a son, and shall name him Emmanuel, which means "God is with us!"*

—ISAIAH 7:14

In announcing the conception of Jesus, God says to all who have ears to hear: "I am not the remote and distant deity you think you worship, but I am with you, in you, around you, before, behind and beside you, closer to you than you are to yourself."

Isaiah 7:10–14; 8:10
Psalm 40
Hebrews 10:4–10
Luke 1:26–38

*O LORD, hear my prayer,*
*and let my cry come to you.*
*Hide not your face from me*
*in the day of my distress.*
*Incline your ear to me;*
*in the day when I call, answer me speedily.*

—PSALM 102:2–3

I have come to realize that when I find myself in distress,
God hasn't hidden away from me or ceased to listen,
however much it might feel like that. The distance I feel
from God at such times is a distance I create myself, by
becoming immersed in myself and trying to solve my
problems in ways that are not God's ways.

Numbers 21:4–9
Psalm 102
John 8:21–30

*If you remain in my word, you will truly be my disciples, and you will know the truth, and the truth will set you free.*

—JOHN 8:31–32

There is a truth that lies deeper than the facts and a freedom that lies deeper than merely being able to do as we please. But we will discover those deeper layers only when we are willing to be at home in God, and not just in our own ego worlds.

Daniel 3:14–20, 91–92, 95
Daniel 3:52–56
John 8:31–42

# MARCH 29

*Look to the LORD in his strength;*
*seek to serve him constantly.*
*Recall the wondrous deeds that he has wrought,*
*his portents, and the judgments he has uttered.*
—PSALM 105:4–5

We don't need to wonder what God's face looks like to seek it. Everyone we meet is made in God's image. Every day that we encounter some of God's faces, we see for ourselves how God's power is at work in the world around us, in all that lives and moves and has its being in God.

Genesis 17:3–9
Psalm 105
John 8:51–59

*I love you, O LORD, my strength,*
*O LORD, my rock, my fortress, my deliverer.*
*My God, my rock of refuge,*
*my shield, the horn of my salvation, my stronghold!*

—PSALM 18:2–3

This is a psalm for the days when we just want to creep into a corner, curl up, and lick our wounds. How good to know that we are not alone in having days like this and that, however remote a corner we find in which to curl up and cry, God will be there waiting to hold us and love us back to life.

Jeremiah 20:10–13
Psalm 18
John 10:31–42

*So the chief priests and the Pharisees convened the Sanhedrin and said, "What are we going to do? This man is performing many signs. If we leave him alone, all will believe in him, and the Romans will come and take away both our land and our nation." But one of them, Caiaphas, who was high priest that year, said to them, "You know nothing, nor do you consider that it is better for you that one man should die instead of the people, so that the whole nation may not perish."*

—JOHN 11:47–50

When we try to do what's best for the majority, we might do great harm to the minorities. This dilemma runs through our governments, societies, and communities. It's a problem that won't go away; our judgment consistently fails to resolve it, perhaps because we need wisdom beyond our scope, yet we don't seek the One who can help.

Ezekiel 37:21–28
Jeremiah 31:10–13
John 11:45–56

*When Jesus and his disciples drew near to Jerusalem, to Bethphage and Bethany at the Mount of Olives, he sent two of his disciples and said to them, "Go into the village opposite you, and immediately on entering it, you will find a colt tethered on which no one has ever sat. Untie it and bring it here."*

—MARK 11:1–2

Jesus rides into the inevitability of death and resurrection, destruction and new creation, on a colt that no one has yet ridden. For me, this is one of the most consoling images in the Gospel stories. Every day, on every new stretch of our personal road, there's a colt no one has ridden, tentatively tethered but ready to carry us into the unknown terrain of tomorrow. Jesus knows this colt, and he rides it with us.

Mark 11:1–10 or John 12:12–16
Isaiah 50:4–7
Psalm 22
Philippians 2:6–11
Mark 14:1–15:47 or Mark 15:1–39

# APRIL 2

*I, the LORD, have called you for the victory of justice,*
*I have grasped you by the hand;*
*I formed you, and set you*
*as a covenant of the people,*
*a light for the nations,*
—ISAIAH 42:6

It isn't hard to recognize that, as "people of the Way," we
are called to serve the cause of right. But there's more to it
than hearing the call. If we respond authentically, God will
ask to take us by the hand and form us for the task. If we
submit to God's formation and guidance, the cause of right
might open up challenges we didn't expect and ones that
we can undertake only in God's power.

Isaiah 42:1–7
Psalm 27
John 12:1–11

*Simon Peter said to him, "Master, where are you going?" Jesus answered him, "Where I am going, you cannot follow me now, though you will follow later." Peter said to him, "Master, why can I not follow you now? I will lay down my life for you." Jesus answered, "Will you lay down your life for me? Amen, amen, I say to you, the cock will not crow before you deny me three times."*

—JOHN 13:36–38

Which of us can say that we've never responded to God as Peter responds to Jesus—overflowing with enthusiasm and convinced that there's nothing he wouldn't do to prove his faith? And then Jesus' voice of realism exposes our immature exuberance: "Far from laying down your life for me, you are very likely to deny even knowing me!" Yet surely he speaks even this hard prophecy more in love than in anger.

Isaiah 49:1–6
Psalm 71
John 13:21–33, 36–38

*The Lord GOD has given me*
*a well-trained tongue,*
*That I might know how to speak to the weary*
*a word that will rouse them.*
*Morning after morning*
*he opens my ear that I may hear.*
—ISAIAH 50:4–5

Sometimes, when faced with another's need, we don't know what to say. The prophet says, "The Lord has given me a well-trained tongue." We immerse ourselves in the Gospels and ask for the grace to internalize Christ's attitudes and values into our specific circumstances. Then, ever so gradually, we may be guided in what to say and in how to respond to whatever situations we encounter.

Isaiah 50:4–9
Psalm 69
Matthew 26:14–25

*Thursday*

# APRIL 5

*If I, therefore, the master and teacher, have washed your feet, you ought to wash one another's feet. I have given you a model to follow, so that as I have done for you, you should also do.*

—JOHN 13:14–15

Through ritual we engage powerfully with the events of our sacred story and help make them present to our daily lives. But our response to this radical call to be servants to one another must go far beyond our annual liturgical ritual. It must go right out into our homes and streets and communities and become a daily reality in all our relationships. Jesus didn't teach his friends how to conduct a ritual but how to live a life.

| **Chrism Mass:** | **Evening Mass of the Lord's Supper:** |
|---|---|
| Isaiah 61:1–3, 6, 8–9 | Exodus 12:1–8, 11–14 |
| Psalm 89 | Psalm 116 |
| Revelation 1:5–8 | 1 Corinthians 11:23–26 |
| Luke 4:16–21 | John 13:1–15 |

*So shall he startle many nations,*
*because of him kings shall stand speechless;*
*for those who have not been told shall see,*
*those who have not heard shall ponder it.*

—ISAIAH 52:15

What the prophet foretold became a living reality, in Christ. The call to follow Jesus turns all our familiar value systems upside down and inside out. If we seriously try to follow where Jesus leads, we will find both hardships and joys that nothing could have prepared us for in advance. Jesus' cross is our crossroad, where we choose either to follow where he leads or to stay where we are comfortable.

Isaiah 52:13—53:12
Psalm 31
Hebrews 4:14–16; 5:7–9
John 18:1–19:42

*They were saying to one another, "Who will roll back the stone for us from the entrance to the tomb?" When they looked up, they saw that the stone had been rolled back; it was very large.*

—MARK 16:3–4

I have spent many sleepless nights worrying about issues that dissolved in the light of day. Holy Saturday might be a good time to bring God any boulders that block our way forward in the path of faith. Alone, we are helpless to move them. In God, all things are possible. And Easter's light may reveal that we created some of those stones.

**Vigil:**

Genesis 1:1–2:2 or Genesis 1:1, 26–31

Psalm 104 or Psalm 33

Genesis 22:1–18 or Genesis 22:1–2, 9–13, 15–18

Psalm 16

Exodus 14:15–15:1

Exodus 15:1–6, 17–18

Isaiah 54:5–14

Psalm 30

Isaiah 55:1–11

Isaiah 12:2–6

Baruch 3:9–15, 32–4:4

Psalm 19

Ezekiel 36:16–28

Psalm 42 or Isaiah 12:2–6 or Psalm 51

Romans 6:3–11

Psalm 118

Mark 16:1–7

*For you have died, and your life is hidden with Christ in God. When Christ your life appears, then you too will appear with him in glory.*

—COLOSSIANS 3:3–4

A heart surgeon once got into an argument with his gardener on the question of souls. "I have cut open hundreds of hearts," he said, "but I have never seen a soul inside them." The gardener replied, "I have accidentally sliced through many daffodil bulbs with my spade, and I have never seen a daffodil inside them."

What is to be is hidden deeply within us and will be revealed only in God's time and through God's power.

Acts 10:34, 37–43
Psalm 118
Colossians 3:1–4 or 1 Corinthians 5:6–8
John 20:1–9 or Mark 16:1–7

*For David says of him:*
*"I saw the Lord ever before me,*
*With him at my right hand I shall not be disturbed.*
*Therefore my heart has been glad and my tongue has exulted."*
—ACTS 2:25–26

Peter is quoting David here, but he is also surely describing his own experience. The terrified disciple—hiding, denying, fleeing—has become the empowered apostle who knows that the one who is always before them cannot be shaken by anything that life or death can do to him. This one truly can release frozen hearts into an eternity of joy.

Acts 2:14, 22–33
Psalm 16
Matthew 28:8–15

# APRIL 10

*Jesus said to her, "Stop holding on to me, for I have not yet ascended to the Father. But go to my brothers and tell them, 'I am going to my Father and your Father, to my God and your God.'" Mary went and announced to the disciples, "I have seen the Lord," and then reported what he had told her.*

—JOHN 20:17–18

Mary Magdalene's joy on meeting the risen Lord must have been overwhelming. "Thank God," she might have said. "The nightmare is over, and we can go back to how things were." "No," Jesus would say. "We can never go back to how things were, but I have lived and died and risen so that together we can walk forward to how things shall become. Don't cling to what you thought you had, but stretch out empty hands to receive all that God is waiting to give you."

Acts 2:36–41

Psalm 33
John 20:11–18

*That very day, the first day of the week, two of Jesus' disciples were going to a village seven miles from Jerusalem called Emmaus, and they were conversing about all the things that had occurred. And it happened that while they were conversing and debating, Jesus himself drew near and walked with them, but their eyes were prevented from recognizing him.*

—LUKE 24:13–16

How often have I missed what God was longing to show me because my gaze was focused only on what I expected to see? How often have I missed God's silent presence because I was too preoccupied with my own affairs? May God give us the grace to expect surprises and the stillness of heart to discover God's constant presence.

Acts 3:1–10
Psalm 105
Luke 24:13–35

*You are the children of the prophets and of the covenant that God made with your ancestors when he said to Abraham, "In your offspring all the families of the earth shall be blessed."*

—ACTS 3:25

Let us never cease to give thanks for all those who have walked the ways of faith before us, guiding and encouraging us on our journey.

And may we, in turn, live in a way that spreads those blessings to all whose lives we touch.

Acts 3:11–26
Psalm 8
Luke 24:35–48

*Jesus said to them, "Children, have you caught anything to eat?"*
*They answered him, "No." So he said to them, "Cast the net over the*
*right side of the boat and you will find something." So they cast it, and*
*were not able to pull it in because of the number of fish.*

—JOHN 21:5–6

Sometimes the smallest adjustment in our point of view—
moving from one side of the boat to the other—can make
a huge difference in our vision. And sometimes it takes an
unexpected stranger on the shore to shift our perspective.

Acts 4:1–12
Psalm 118
John 21:1–14

*But later, as the Eleven were at table, he appeared to them and rebuked them for their unbelief and hardness of heart because they had not believed those who saw him after he had been raised. He said to them, "Go into the whole world and proclaim the Gospel to every creature."*

—MARK 16:14–15

It seems a bit harsh that Jesus reproached the eleven for their reluctance to believe in this miracle of all miracles. Yet Jesus' reproach rapidly turned into a new commandment. In spite of their weakness and incredulity, he trusts the apostles with the great commission of proclaiming the Good News to all creation. He calls us, and trusts us, to do likewise.

Acts 4:13–21
Psalm 118
Mark 16:9–15

*Jesus came and stood in their midst and said to them, "Peace be with you." When he had said this, he showed them his hands and his side. The disciples rejoiced when they saw the Lord. Jesus said to them again, "Peace be with you. As the Father has sent me, so I send you."*

—JOHN 20:19–21

Jesus loves paradox, for paradox is the language of the soul. In this incident, peace flowed out of woundedness and agony, and in its turn, peace became the source of action and mission.

Acts 4:32–35
Psalm 118
1 John 5:1–6
John 20:19–31

*"Why did the Gentiles rage
and the peoples entertain folly?
The kings of the earth took their stand
and the princes gathered together
against the Lord and against his anointed."*

—ACTS 4:25–26

Centuries ago, the Gentiles raged and the peoples
entertained folly. Today, the rage and folly have not
diminished, nor have we ceased to plot one against another,
to undermine the way of life of other peoples, and to set
out upon wars again and again. In doing so, we act against
God.

Acts 4:23–31
Psalm 2
John 3:1–8

*The community of believers was of one heart and mind, and no one claimed that any of his possessions was his own, but they had everything in common. With great power the Apostles bore witness to the resurrection of the Lord Jesus, and great favor was accorded them all.*

—ACTS 4:32–33

When we are truly united, heart and soul, with another person or group of people—for example, in a loving family—we don't think twice about sharing everything we have with one another. Unfortunately, such a degree of unity is in extremely short supply on planet Earth. Yet every selfless act and every compassionate word make deep unity a bit more possible.

Acts 4:32–37
Psalm 93
John 3:7–15

*Filled with jealousy, [the Sadducees] laid hands upon the Apostles and put them in the public jail. But during the night, the angel of the Lord opened the doors of the prison, led them out, and said, "Go and take your place in the temple area, and tell the people everything about this life." When they heard this, they went to the temple early in the morning and taught.*

—ACTS 5:17–21

Jealousy can imprison us in bonds of anger and resentment. Do any chains chafe your wrists and ankles? What kind of angel do you need to set you free, and can you ask the Lord to send an angel? Freed of jealousy, the human heart can expand into a courageous new joy.

Acts 5:17–26
Psalm 34
John 3:16–21

*For the one whom God sent speaks the words of God. He does not ration his gift of the Spirit. The Father loves the Son and has given everything over to him. Whoever believes in the Son has eternal life, but whoever disobeys the Son will not see life.*

—JOHN 3:34–36

These gifts of God are without limits, the Spirit given with nothing held back. In God's economy there is nothing put aside for a rainy day. God's love is poured out totally. Ours is not a God of caution or hesitation, and the response this God calls forth from us is to be equally all-or-nothing.

Acts 5:27–33
Psalm 34
John 3:31–36

*"There is a boy here who has five barley loaves and two fish; but what good are these for so many?" . . . Then Jesus took the loaves, gave thanks, and distributed them to those who were reclining, and also as much of the fish as they wanted.*

—JOHN 6:9, 11

Jesus seems to relish little things: a mustard seed, a widow's mite and, here, a little boy's lunch. The One who created a universe from nothing has no problem turning a sandwich into a feast. What Jesus does with the loaves and fishes he does with the meager offerings of our lives, too, if we offer them in love and hold nothing back.

Acts 5:34–42
Psalm 27
John 6:1–15

# APRIL 21

*It had already grown dark, and Jesus had not yet come to them. The sea was stirred up because a strong wind was blowing. When they had rowed about three or four miles, they saw Jesus walking on the sea and coming near the boat.*

—JOHN 6:17–19

Jesus never promised us an easy ride, never said that the winds and storms and darkness we fear wouldn't come upon us. He did promise, though, that whatever happens, he will be right there with us, in the same boat.

Acts 6:1–7
Psalm 33
John 6:16–21

*Now I know, brothers, that you acted out of ignorance,*
*just as your leaders did; but God has thus brought to fulfillment*
*what he had announced beforehand.*

—ACTS 3:17–18

Can you imagine God saying this to you, in your time and place: "I know, friends, that neither you nor your leaders had any idea what you were really doing. Nevertheless, I am weaving my dream for creation with all the broken threads of your faults and failures, for nothing you ever do, or fail to do, can undermine my dream."

Acts 3:13–15, 17–19
Psalm 4
1 John 2:1–5
Luke 24:35–48

*So they said to him, "What can we do to accomplish the works of God?" Jesus answered and said to them, "This is the work of God, that you believe in the one he sent."*

—JOHN 6:28–29

Human beings, especially in the Western world, are turning into human *doings*. Today's reading reminds us that, in our own strength, there is no way we can do God's works. Instead, working for God is fundamentally about believing, and *believing* really means trusting. When we entrust ourselves and all that we do to God, then God can work in and through us. Without trust, all our efforts are simply self-serving.

Acts 6:8–15
Psalm 119
John 6:22–29

*As they were stoning Stephen, he called out, "Lord Jesus, receive my spirit." Then he fell to his knees and cried out in a loud voice, "Lord, do not hold this sin against them."*

—ACTS 7:59–60

Stephen's message is echoed by many people in our own century whose lives have been grievously harmed by crimes and atrocities committed against them: If you hold on to anger and bitterness you will only continue to harm your own soul, but if you can let it go and surrender the desire for revenge or retribution, you will free your soul to move on.

Acts 7:51–8:1
Psalm 31
John 6:30–35

*Jesus appeared to the Eleven and said to them: "Go into the whole world and proclaim the Gospel to every creature."*

—MARK 16:14–15

Disciples are people who learn from everything the teacher shows them. Apostles are people who are then sent out to share with the wider world all they have learned. We are all called to learn, and to keep on learning, as disciples. We are all sent out as apostles, to share what we have been given.

1 Peter 5:5–14
Psalm 89
Mark 16:15–20

*Jesus said to the crowds: "No one can come to me unless the Father who sent me draw him, and I will raise him on the last day."*

—JOHN 6:44

Today's Scripture shows such a gentle, powerful image: being *drawn* by the Father, like a precious treasure, drawn home by a golden cord, or a sliver of iron drawn toward a mighty magnet. This is the God who attracts, not a god who coerces.

Acts 8:26–40
Psalm 66
John 6:44–51

*So Ananias went and entered the house; laying his hands on him, he said, "Saul, my brother, the Lord has sent me, Jesus who appeared to you on the way by which you came, that you may regain your sight and be filled with the Holy Spirit." Immediately things like scales fell from his eyes and he regained his sight.*

—ACTS 9:17–18

The courage of Ananias never fails to amaze me. Asked by God to confront Saul, the ruthless persecutor of the fledgling Christians, Ananias took his life in his hands and approached Saul, public enemy number one. It took both Ananias's courage and obedience and the power of the Holy Spirit to cause the scales to fall off of Saul's eyes. Whenever any of us responds to God with courage and obedience, it makes a difference for all of us and opens the door to the miracle.

Acts 9:1–20
Psalm 117
John 6:52–59

*How shall I make a return to the LORD*
*for all the good he has done for me?*
*The cup of salvation I will take up,*
*and I will call upon the name*
*of the LORD.*

—PSALM 116:12–13

We can never pay back God's love for us, but we can pay it forward, not only by partaking of the cup of salvation ourselves but also by sharing it freely, without reservation or exclusion, with all our brothers and sisters who long for the taste of God.

Acts 9:31–42
Psalm 116
John 6:60–69

*Beloved, we are God's children now; what we shall be has not yet been revealed. We do know that when it is revealed we shall be like him, for we shall see him as he is.*

—1 JOHN 3:2

When we look into a mirror we see only an image of ourselves, distorted by sin and selfishness, and sometimes we don't much like what we see. When the moment comes to look upon the fullness of God's being, then we will see not only God but also ourselves as we truly are, as God created us to be: human images of Godself.

Acts 4:8–12
Psalm 118
1 John 3:1–2
John 10:11–18

*But whoever enters through the gate is the shepherd of the sheep.*
*The gatekeeper opens it for him, and the sheep hear his voice, as he calls*
*his own sheep by name and leads them out.*

—JOHN 10:2–3

Amid the clamor of so many inauthentic voices demanding
our attention, how will we recognize the true voice, the
voice of the shepherd? Gradually, perhaps, as we sift through
the memories of our daily experience, we will begin to
notice the voice that alone resonates with the core of our
soul, the voice that calls us and empowers us to become the
best that we can be, the voice that warns us when we are
going off course, the voice that assures us of God's unfailing
love. This art of reflective living is the project of a lifetime,
which we work out hour by hour and day by day.

Acts 11:1–18
Psalms 42, 43
John 10:1–10

*The works I do in my Father's name testify to me. But you do not
believe, because you are not among my sheep.*

—JOHN 10:25–26

We know it is the Shepherd who is present when we see
the effects of his presence: peace, justice, integrity, and
love. And when these effects resonate in our hearts, we can
be reassured that we are his sheep.

Acts 11:19–26
Psalm 87
John 10:22–30

*And if anyone hears my words and does not observe them, I do not condemn him, for I did not come to condemn the world but to save the world. Whoever rejects me and does not accept my words has something to judge him: the word that I spoke, it will condemn him on the last day.*

—JOHN 12:47–48

Whenever I act or speak against the promptings of my own conscience and integrity, the turmoil that follows comes not from other people, let alone from God, but from the sense of being dislocated from my own soul. I become my own judge and jury, often more ready to condemn myself than I am to hear the promise of Jesus, who comes not to condemn but to make whole.

Acts 12:24–13:5
Psalm 67
John 12:44–50

*Not a word nor a discourse*
*whose voice is not heard;*
*Through all the earth their voice resounds,*
*and to the ends of the world, their message.*

—PSALM 19:3–4

The lives of those who live close to God's heart and live
God's life in this world are like stones thrown into a pool.
The ripples of their goodness, trust, and faithfulness spread
out in ever-widening circles until the whole earth
is touched and changed by their example.

1 Corinthians 15:1–8
Psalm 19
John 14:6–14

*We ourselves are proclaiming this good news to you that what God promised our fathers he has brought to fulfillment for us, their children, by raising up Jesus.*

—ACTS 13:32–33

The journey of faith is not a succession of individual sprints to salvation, but a continuous process, a relay race in which every generation strives to live by the light of God and pass on its experience and wisdom to those who follow after. In this way, age after age, the whole human family moves closer toward its destiny in God.

Acts 13:26–33
Psalm 2
John 14:1–6

*Amen, amen, I say to you, whoever believes in me will do the works that
I do, and will do greater ones than these, because I am going
to the Father.*

—JOHN 14:12

Jesus, the fulfillment of everything that it means to be
human, the Omega of evolution, is also the beginning
of our journey toward that fulfillment. He shows us who
we can become; he is the Alpha of our adventure into
our true destiny.

Acts 13:44–52
Psalm 98
John 14:7–14

*Children, let us love not in word or speech but in deed and truth.*

*Now this is how we shall know that we belong to the truth.*
—1 JOHN 3:18–19

Anyone who has been involved in raising children knows all too well that children are much more likely to copy what you do than listen to what you say. Words can deceive, but our actions tell the truth about our intentions.

Acts 9:26–31
Psalm 22
1 John 3:18–24
John 15:1–8

*Not to us, O LORD, not to us*
*but to your name give glory*
*because of your mercy, because of your truth.*
*Why should the pagans say,*
*"Where is their God?"*
—PSALM 115:1–2

Michael is a very gifted jazz pianist, but he is always at the back of the stage when the quintet performs, and the audience rarely sees him in action. When an admirer commented on this and regretted Michael's low profile, he replied without a moment's hesitation: "But I am here to serve the music. The music isn't here to serve me."

Acts 14:5–18
Psalm 115
John 14:21–26

*Jesus said to his disciples: "Peace I leave with you; my peace I give to you. Not as the world gives do I give it to you. Do not let your hearts be troubled or afraid."*

—JOHN 14:27

God's peace goes far beyond the absence of conflict. It is a wholeness, an integrity, a togetherness that cannot be fragmented by anything life throws at us. God's peace is the free gift of the One who is that perfect wholeness, and we can't obtain it from any other source.

Acts 14:19–28
Psalm 145
John 14:27–31

*Jesus said to his disciples: "I am the true vine, and my Father is the vine grower. He takes away every branch in me that does not bear fruit, and everyone that does he prunes so that it bears more fruit."*

—JOHN 15:1–2

I can imagine a vine on a Californian hillside, shivering now that the vine grower has just stripped it of the dead wood. Perhaps it feels the sting of reproach and the pain of punishment in the vinedresser's shears. Perhaps it feels it has failed. If only it could see into the next season of growth, and how fruitful it will become because the vinedresser has pruned it. Perhaps that vine is me—or you?

Acts 15:1–6
Psalm 122
John 15:1–8

*If you keep my commandments, you will remain in my love, just as I have kept my Father's commandments and remain in his love.*

*I have told you this so that my joy might be in you and your joy might be complete.*

—JOHN 15:10–11

As little children, we do what our parents tell us because we want them to keep on loving us. But as we grow older, if we live in a loving family, we realize that our parents' love is always there. Indeed, we have our very existence in their love. From then on, we do what they ask because of the love that binds us to others. Only then can real joy begin to flow.

Acts 15:7–21
Psalm 96
John 15:9–11

*My heart is steadfast, O God; my heart is steadfast;*
*I will sing and chant praise.*
*Awake, O my soul; awake lyre and harp!*
*I will wake the dawn.*
—PSALM 57:8–9

Every time we give expression to what is in our hearts—
personal love for another, or an inspiration that becomes
a poem or a painting, or a creative desire that becomes
a beautiful garden or a shared meal or a child's birthday
cake, or an impulse for justice that becomes a voice of
protest or a demand for reform—we wake the dawn and
move all of humanity another day closer to its fulfillment.

Acts 15:22–31
Psalm 57
John 15:12–17

---

⋑ 167 ⋐

*The LORD is good:*
*his kindness endures forever,*
*and his faithfulness, to all generations.*
—PSALM 100:5

I think of a wise friend, now approaching his nineties.
I think of how he always sees the good in others and never
comments on the less than good. I think of how ready he
is to let go of past hurts and grudges and of what a big
heart he has, even to those who have harmed him. I think
of how he is quite simply always there, a steady rock in a
turbulent world. Goodness, mercy, and faithfulness—these
are reflections of God in human hearts and lives.

Acts 16:1–10
Psalm 100
John 15:18–21

*It was not you who chose me, but I who chose you and appointed you to go and bear fruit that will remain.*

—JOHN 15:16

I have often noticed that the projects I initiate myself, even when I think they are good, rarely bear fruit and seem to dry up after a short time. Those undertakings that take me by surprise, however, the ones that seem to choose me, often bear fruit that I could not have envisioned.

Acts 10:25–26, 34–35, 44–48
Psalm 98
1 John 4:7–10
John 15:9–17

---

*From the rising to the setting of the sun*
*is the name of the LORD to be praised.*
*High above all nations is the LORD;*
*above the heavens is his glory.*

—PSALM 113:3–4

To fly above the clouds and follow the sun from its rising in the east to its setting in the west is to gain a glimpse of God's glory, of which the psalmist speaks. We, however, land at our destination airport, travel weary and jet lagged. God alone never wearies, and the sun of God's love never sets. A saint is one who has grasped something of the measure of God's love and allows it to be reflected in his or her own life.

Acts 1:15–17, 20–26
Psalm 113
John 15:9–17

*But I tell you the truth, it is better for you that I go. For if I do not go, the Advocate will not come to you. But if I go, I will send him to you.*

—JOHN 16:7

Sometimes we have to let go of what we think we can't possibly live without, to be freed to receive the very gift that will give us life.

Acts 16:22–34
Psalm 138
John 16:5–11

*Jesus said to his disciples: "I have much more to tell you, but you cannot bear it now. But when he comes, the Spirit of truth, he will guide you to all truth."*

—JOHN 16:12–13

We might say that Jesus took his friends to the end of their spiritual childhood and, in his earthly life, taught them as much as they were capable of learning. On the threshold of their spiritual coming-of-age, he sent his Spirit to accompany and empower them as they lived out the consequences of their commitment and grew into the fullness of his truth.

Acts 17:15, 22–18:1
Psalm 148
John 16:12–15

*May the God of our Lord Jesus Christ, the Father of glory, give you a spirit of wisdom and revelation resulting in knowledge of him. May the eyes of your hearts be enlightened, that you may know what is the hope that belongs to his call.*

—EPHESIANS 1:17–18

It is a paradox, but Jesus has to disappear from sight before the inner eyes of his friends will fully open, before they understand who he really is and what his life, death, and resurrection really mean for them.

May we, too, ask for the grace today to go beyond what we can see with our eyes to what only the heart can see.

Acts 1:1–11
Psalm 47
Ephesians 1:17–23 or 4:1–13 or 4:1–7, 11–13
Mark 16:15–20

---

*So you also are now in anguish. But I will see you again, and your*
*hearts will rejoice, and no one will take your joy away from you.*
*On that day you will not question me about anything.*

—JOHN 16:22–23

Most of us are probably bursting with questions we would
want to ask Jesus if we could meet him face-to-face. But
that is now. John tells us that when time dissolves into
eternity, there will be no more questions because our
understanding will be opened fully to the truth and we will
see our passing sorrows as merely the labor pains
of an unending joy.

Acts 18:9–18
Psalm 47
John 16:20–23

*I have told you this in figures of speech. The hour is coming when
I will no longer speak to you in figures but I will tell you clearly
about the Father.*

—JOHN 16:25

Metaphors are keys that can open small doorways into
the meaning of the Mystery. Now, as Jesus returns to the
Father, he has himself become the key that opens up the
Mystery for us all—and makes all other keys redundant.

Acts 18:23–28
Psalm 47
John 16:23–28

*No one has ever seen God. Yet, if we love one another, God remains in us, and his love is brought to perfection in us.*

—1 JOHN 4:12

No one has ever seen God. No one has ever seen love. To trust that all existence has life and meaning in and through divine love is our act of faith. Every time we relate to one another in loving ways, those acts of faith become incarnate in our lives and move humanity toward completeness.

Acts 1:15–17, 20–26
Psalm 103
1 John 4:11–16
John 17:11–19

*Behold, the hour is coming and has arrived when each of you will be scattered to his own home and you will leave me alone. But I am not alone, because the Father is with me. I have told you this so that you might have peace in me.*

—JOHN 16:32–33

A theme song of fans of the soccer team in Liverpool, United Kingdom, includes the words: "Walk on, walk on with hope in your heart, and you'll never walk alone." Jesus makes us the same promise. We will be scattered, and each of us will be challenged to walk our unique pathway through life. Yet in our hearts, we carry the very presence of the One in whom we are all one. *Alone* becomes *all one*. The transformation happens through faith, which gives hope and leads to love.

Acts 19:1–8
Psalm 68
John 16:29–33

*I pray for them. I do not pray for the world but for the ones you have given me, because they are yours, and everything of mine is yours and everything of yours is mine, and I have been glorified in them. And now I will no longer be in the world, but they are in the world, while I am coming to you.*

—JOHN 17:9–11

Jesus, the one who walks in the world, is also the one who dwells eternally in God. Today, and every day, he prays for us. We have not yet crossed the bridge into the fullness of God's presence. He knows where we are and how we feel, and he brings us constantly to the Father's heart, in prayer.

Acts 20:17–27
Psalm 68
John 17:1–11

*And now I commend you to God and to that gracious word of his that can build you up.*

—ACTS 20:32

The Word, that was in the beginning, the Word that brought forth all creation, is the same Word that continues to hold each of us in existence and build us up into the fullness of our calling.

Acts 20:28–38
Psalm 68
John 17:11–19

*[I pray] . . . that they may all be one, as you, Father,
are in me and I in you.*

—JOHN 17:21

We are like the spokes of a wheel; each of us mainly is
concerned with running our own life. Individually, we are
ineffective, but when we come together—joined to God at
the center and linked to one another at the rim—then, and
only then, will the wheel move forward.

Acts 22:30; 23:6–11
Psalm 16
John 17:20–26

*[Jesus] said to [Peter] the third time, "Simon, son of John, do you love me?" Peter was distressed that he had said to him a third time, "Do you love me?" and he said to him, "Lord, you know everything; you know that I love you." Jesus said to him, "Feed my sheep."*

—JOHN 21:17

Declarations of love, however passionate and well intended, amount to nothing if they don't translate into loving service to the beloved.

Acts 25:13–21
Psalm 103
John 21:15–19

⇒ 181 ⇐

*It is on account of the hope of Israel that I wear these chains.*

—ACTS 28:20

When the Holy Spirit fills us and reshapes our lives, chains
that have held us captive can be transformed into links of
love and hope, challenging us to come out of the captivity of
fear and timidity and embrace the challenge to speak truth
by the authority of the One whose Spirit empowers us.

Acts 28:16–20, 30–31
Psalm 11
John 21:20–25

*And they were all filled with the Holy Spirit and began to speak in
different tongues, as the Spirit enabled them to proclaim.*

—ACTS 2:4

The most effective way to learn a foreign language is by
total immersion, which requires us to surrender completely
to the new language and cease to think and speak in our
own. Pentecost is a total immersion experience that fills
us with the Spirit, who pours out of us in words everyone
can hear and in ways that apply perfectly to each person's
specific needs.

**Vigil:**
Genesis 11:1–9 or Exodus 19:3–8, 16–20,
or Ezekiel 37:1–14 or Joel 3:1–5
Psalm 104
Romans 8:22–27
John 7:37–39
**Extended Vigil:**
Genesis 11:1–9
Exodus 19:3–8, 16–20
Ezekiel 37:1–14

Joel 3:1–5
Psalm 104
Romans 8:22–27
John 7:37–39
**Day:**
Acts 2:1–11
Psalm 104
1 Corinthians 12:3–7, 12–13, or Galatians
5:16–25
John 20:19–23 or John 15:26–27; 16:12–15

*Although you have not seen him you love him; even though you do not
see him now yet you believe in him, you rejoice with an indescribable
and glorious joy.*

—1 PETER 1:8

When I saw the first ultrasound image of my unborn
grandchild, when she was just an inch long, a pang of love
and joy quivered through my heart. It was the beginning
of a love that would grow and grow through all the years
to come. It reminds me that love is possible long before the
beloved can be seen and touched and that we who have
never seen Jesus can nevertheless love him and follow him
with unfailing joy, because his imprint is on our hearts.

1 Peter 1:3–9
Psalm 111
Mark 10:17–27

*But many that are first will be last, and the last will be first.*

—MARK 10:31

A boy who is bullied at school and retreats into his private world of music confounds all expectations by emerging as a gifted, world-class tenor.

A child who has been labeled "learning impaired" and feels rejected by her classmates surprises everyone by rushing to help a classmate who has fallen into a lake.

God delights in confronting us by putting first those whom we consider last.

1 Peter 1:10–16
Psalm 98
Mark 10:28–31

*All flesh is like grass,*
*and all its glory like the flower of the field;*
*the grass withers,*
*and the flower wilts;*
*but the word of the Lord remains forever.*
—1 PETER 1:24–25

There is sadness when the last leaves fall from the trees as winter approaches. Sadness when the cherry blossom fades and falls. But the roots remain, untouched by the fading and falling. The roots remain, gestating next year's growth.

1 Peter 1:18–25
Psalm 147
Mark 10:32–45

*God indeed is my savior,*
*I am confident and unafraid.*
*My strength and my courage is the LORD,*
*and he has been my savior.*
*With joy you will draw water*
*at the fountain of salvation.*

—ISAIAH 12:2–3

Perhaps Mary seeks out Elizabeth in trepidation about what is happening to her. Perhaps Elizabeth shares her own anxieties about bringing a child into the world. Yet today we celebrate their joy, which overrode their fears, and we reflect on the prophet's promise that joy, not fear, will define all that is to come—a joy that God's dream is unfolding as it should, because of their obedience and trust.

Zephaniah 3:14–18 or Romans 12:9–16
Isaiah 12:2–6
Luke 1:39–56

*Beloved: The end of all things is at hand. Therefore be serious and sober-minded so that you will be able to pray. Above all, let your love for one another be intense, because love covers a multitude of sins.*

—1 PETER 4:7–8

When everything seems to be going wrong, and our neatly ordered lives are collapsing in a heap around us, two things matter, and two things only: to stay in touch with the deep center of stillness in the depths of our hearts, where God is indwelling, and to keep doing the more loving thing, however we may feel.

1 Peter 4:7–13
Psalm 96
Mark 11:11–26

*Keep yourselves in the love of God and wait for the mercy of our Lord Jesus Christ that leads to eternal life.*

—JUDE 21

A chick can't determine the hour of its hatching, as it lies curled up inside its egg. An acorn cannot, of itself, become an oak tree.

The life which is our eternal destiny is revealed only through waiting, with a responsive, attentive heart, for God's grace to break open the shell of our helplessness.

Jude 17, 20–25
Psalm 63
Mark 11:27–33

*For you did not receive a spirit of slavery to fall back into fear, but you received a Spirit of adoption, through whom we cry, "Abba, Father!"*
—ROMANS 8:15

God is love, and anything that imprisons us in unhealthy fear or exploits our fears to seduce us into uncritical obedience is not of God. It is of the spirit of fear, which is love's opposite; it is the spirit that enslaves, not the spirit that liberates.

Deuteronomy 4:32–34, 39–40
Psalm 33
Romans 8:14–17
Matthew 28:16–20

*For this very reason, make every effort to supplement your faith with virtue, virtue with knowledge, knowledge with self-control, self-control with endurance, endurance with devotion, devotion with mutual affection, mutual affection with love.*

—2 PETER 1:5–7

It is said that the longest journey is the one from the head to the heart. Today's reading shows another version of that journey: from the foundation of faith to the fullness of love. Every time we choose the way of goodness, every time we seek to deepen our understanding, every time we exercise patience and act out of kindness, we make a personal step that moves us from merely professing our faith to living it through a life of love.

2 Peter 1:2–7
Psalm 91
Mark 12:1–12

*But according to his promise we await new heavens and a new earth in which righteousness dwells.*

—2 PETER 3:13

Jim had always resented his disabled younger brother, and they often quarreled. After his brother's premature death, Jim was stricken with remorse for his unloving behavior, and he longed to ask his brother for forgiveness. One night, perhaps in a dream, perhaps in prayer, he saw his brother, quite perfect and free of all disability. They embraced for a moment, and it lasted for eternity. From that moment on, Jim knew beyond all question the reality of what Peter tells us today.

2 Peter 3:12–15, 17–18
Psalm 90
Mark 12:13–17

*For God did not give us a spirit of cowardice but rather of power and love and self-control.*

—2 TIMOTHY 1:7

Power and love and self-control—those are not three companions we often find walking side by side. Power can destroy the one who wields it if it is not exercised in love. Love can become possessive if it is not offered in a spirit of self-control. When we are called out of our protective shell of timidity, we are called to speak truth to power, but to do so in love and with self-control—a gift that only the Spirit can give.

2 Timothy 1:1–3, 6–12
Psalm 123
Mark 12:18–27

*"To love [God] with all your heart, with all your understanding, with all your strength, and to love your neighbor as yourself" is worth more than all burnt offerings and sacrifices.*

—MARK 12:33

To love in the way this Gospel story describes is much harder than mere religious observance. Perhaps that is why we so often emphasize the importance of religious observance, sometimes at the expense of love.

2 Timothy 2:8–15
Psalm 25
Mark 12:28–34

*In fact, all who want to live religiously in Christ Jesus*
*will be persecuted.*

—2 TIMOTHY 3:12

Sometimes it amazes me how much can go wrong before
an event that promises to be good for us spiritually.
The car breaks down, keys go missing, your back goes out.
It's always a sure sign to me that the destructive spirits are
feeling threatened, because God is going to be active in
the event.

2 Timothy 3:10–17
Psalm 119
Mark 12:35–37

*Beware of the scribes, who like to go around in long robes and accept greetings in the marketplaces, seats of honor in synagogues, and places of honor at banquets. They devour the houses of widows and, as a pretext, recite lengthy prayers.*

—MARK 12:38–40

If we meet the scribes in our own time and place, let us remember Jesus' warning. If we meet the scribes in ourselves, in our own characteristics, let us ask God to hold up the mirror of truth so that we see ourselves as God sees us.

2 Timothy 4:1–8
Psalm 71
Mark 12:38–44

*Amen, I say to you, I shall not drink again the fruit of the vine until the day when I drink it new in the kingdom of God.*

—MARK 14:25

The poignancy of the final moments in another person's life can seem unbearable. We know that we are doing things with them for the last time, and we have an agonizing awareness that nothing will be the same again. In today's reading, Jesus takes his friends through that frightening void between all that has been and all that shall be. He helps them let go, but he also invites them to look toward a future they cannot imagine. What he does for them, he does for us every time we take anxious but necessary steps over the threshold and away from the familiar.

Exodus 24:3–8
Psalm 116
Hebrews 9:11–15
Mark 14:12–16, 22–26

*Do not take gold or silver or copper for your belts; no sack for the journey, or a second tunic, or sandals, or walking stick.*
*The laborer deserves his keep.*

—MATTHEW 10:9–10

A friend of mine, a Franciscan sister, used to travel lightly, with only a small bag, a change of clothes, and her Bible. One day she was checking in at Heathrow Airport to fly to Australia. The check-in attendant weighed her small bag and asked, "Where is your checked baggage?" My friend replied, "This is all I have." The check-in attendant gazed at her incredulously and then commented, "How I wish I could travel like that!"

Acts 11:21–26; 13:1–3
Psalm 98
Matthew 10:7–13

*The jar of flour shall not go empty, nor the jug of oil run dry,*
*until the day when the LORD sends rain upon the earth.*

—1 KINGS 17:14

The poverty-stricken widow gave Elijah her last handful of meal and a little oil in a jug. She gave all she had, and with it, she gave away her own last meal. In the paradox of our life in God, when we surrender all we think we have, we discover inexhaustible supplies of what we truly need.

1 Kings 17:7–16
Psalm 4
Matthew 5:13–16

*Jesus said to his disciples: "Do not think that I have come to abolish the law or the prophets. I have come not to abolish but to fulfill."*

—MATTHEW 5:17

Everything new is built on all that went before. If we disregard that wisdom, we are in danger of cutting off the branch we are sitting on.

1 Kings 18:20–39
Psalm 16
Matthew 5:17–19

*Thus you have prepared the land:*
*drenching its furrows, breaking up its clods,*
*Softening it with showers,*
*blessing its yield.*
—PSALM 65:10–11

How readily we curse the showers that rain on our parade,
the unwanted interruptions to the smooth running of our
lives. The psalmist reminds us that the same showers are
essential to our growth and soften our hearts to receive
fresh blessings.

1 Kings 18:41–46
Psalm 65
Matthew 5:20–26

*[May God] grant you in accord with the riches of his glory to be strengthened with power through his Spirit in the inner self, and that Christ may dwell in your hearts through faith.*

—EPHESIANS 3:16–17

When we remember those who have gone ahead of us, what is their true legacy? It's not necessarily their achievements or their ideas. What lives on is the love they shared with us, a love that has shaped us and bonded us together for all eternity. It is the heart, not the head, that becomes the channel of eternal life.

Hosea 11:1, 3–4, 8–9
Isaiah 12:2–6
Ephesians 3:8–12, 14–19
John 19:31–37

# JUNE 16

*Elijah set out, and came upon Elisha, son of Shaphat, as he was plowing with twelve yoke of oxen; he was following the twelfth. Elijah went over to him and threw his cloak over him.*

—1 KINGS 19:19

Each one of us plows the furrow of our life behind "twelve yoke of oxen" who go before us—the men and women who have guided us, whether long past or still present. Who do you see plowing the furrow ahead of you? To whom do you want to say, "Thank you"?

1 Kings 19:19–21
Psalm 16
Luke 2:41–51

# JUNE 17

*Jesus said to the crowds, "This is how it is with the kingdom of God; it is as if a man were to scatter seed on the land and would sleep and rise night and day and through it all the seed would sprout and grow, he knows not how. Of its own accord the land yields fruit, first the blade, then the ear, then the full grain in the ear."*

—MARK 4:26–28

God doesn't need our help to grow God's kingdom on the earth. All God needs is the soil of our hearts in which to plant the seed and our willingness to watch and wait and tend its growth until the fruits appear.

Ezekiel 17:22–24
Psalm 92
2 Corinthians 5:6–10
Mark 4:26–34

# JUNE 18

*Should anyone press you into service for one mile,*
*go with him for two miles.*
—MATTHEW 5:41

What we do under compulsion can disempower us and
be counterproductive. What we do freely empowers us
and often bears rich fruit. Jesus urges us to go beyond
compulsion to freedom, beyond obligation to joy,
beyond law to love.

1 Kings 21:1–16
Psalm 5
Matthew 5:38–42

*Jesus said to his disciples: "You have heard that it was said, 'You shall love your neighbor and hate your enemy.' But I say to you, love your enemies, and pray for those who persecute you."*

—MATTHEW 5:43–44

Jesus' words to his disciples sound so impossible, so impractical, that we can easily dismiss them as hopeless idealism. But if we unpack the command to love our enemies and translate it not so much as "have loving feelings for them" but as "act in the most loving way you can toward them," then the challenge looks rather different.

1 Kings 21:17–29
Psalm 51
Matthew 5:43–48

*But when you give alms, do not let your left hand know what your right is doing, so that your almsgiving may be secret. And your Father who sees in secret will repay you.*

—MATTHEW 6:3–4

A little stream flowed into a rushing river. No one saw it. No one heard it. Yet this gift enriched both the stream and the river, and the ocean welcomed them together when they arrived. May the gifts we give to life and to one another be just as quiet and unnoticed, and just as fruitful.

2 Kings 2:1, 6–14
Psalm 31
Matthew 6:1–6, 16–18

*Jesus said to his disciples, "In praying, do not babble like the pagans, who think that they will be heard because of their many words. Do not be like them. Your Father knows what you need before you ask him."*

—MATTHEW 6:7–8

May there be a little silence in our homes so that we might hear the cries of one another's hearts. May there be a little silence in our places of worship so that we might hear the quiet movements of our God. May there be a little silence in our lives so that we might be still and know.

Sirach 48:1–14
Psalm 97
Matthew 6:7–15

---

*Jesus said to his disciples: "Do not store up for yourselves treasures on earth, where moth and decay destroy, and thieves break in and steal. But store up treasures in heaven, where neither moth nor decay destroys, nor thieves break in and steal. For where your treasure is, there also will your heart be."*

—MATTHEW 6:19–21

If we invest our treasure in Wall Street and our heart's
energy with it, can our hearts live in heaven?

2 Kings 11:1–4, 9–18, 20
Psalm 132
Matthew 6:19–23

*Do not worry about tomorrow; tomorrow will take care of itself.*
*Sufficient for a day is its own evil.*

—MATTHEW 6:34

It has been wisely said that life is what happens when you are busy making plans for something else. Let us not allow today to pass us by, by losing ourselves in our hopes and fears about tomorrow.

2 Chronicles 24:17–25
Psalm 89
Matthew 6:24–34

# JUNE 24

• THE NATIVITY OF ST. JOHN THE BAPTIST •

*From this man's descendants God, according to his promise, has brought to Israel a savior, Jesus. John heralded his coming by proclaiming a baptism of repentance to all the people of Israel.*

—ACTS 13:23–24

Heralds are usually flamboyant. They alert us to coming events of great importance. John will be a different kind of herald. He will call people out to the desert, away from the bustle and noise of the cities, to reflect in the quiet on what they need to do, to prepare for the One who is coming. Today we celebrate John's birth, knowing that, after he fulfilled his task, he suffered a cruel and untimely death. The herald gave way to the Good News he foretold.

| **Vigil:** | **Day:** |
|:---:|:---:|
| Jeremiah 1:4–10 | Isaiah 49:1–6 |
| Psalm 71 | Psalm 139 |
| 1 Peter 1:8–12 | Acts 13:22–26 |
| Luke 1:5–17 | Luke 1:57–66, 80 |

*Stop judging, that you may not be judged. For as you judge,*
*so will you be judged, and the measure with which you measure will be*
*measured out to you.*

—MATTHEW 7:1–2

I have a boomerang on my wall, a souvenir from Australia.
I half expect it to go flying back to Brisbane on its own
one of these days. The boomerang is a daily reminder
that whenever I send a destructive or unloving thought or
action to the people around me, I myself will be caught
eventually in its negative backlash. But whenever I send a
gesture of gratitude or a touch of compassion, those gifts
will return to enrich my own soul.

2 Kings 17:5–8, 13–15, 18
Psalm 60
Matthew 7:1–5

*Enter through the narrow gate; for the gate is wide and the road broad
that leads to destruction, and those who enter through it are many.
How narrow the gate and constricted the road that leads to life.
And those who find it are few.*

—MATTHEW 7:13–14

The narrow path of life is strewn with stones. It demands
hard choices, acts of sacrifice, and a willingness to let go of
what we think we can't live without. It is a hard path, but
every stone along it takes us closer to the mountaintop.

The wide path is much easier, much less challenging. It lets
us live for ourselves and avoid many of the stones, but it
will never lead us up the mountain.

2 Kings 19:9–11, 14–21, 31–36
Psalm 48
Matthew 7:6, 12–14

*A good tree cannot bear bad fruit, nor can a rotten tree bear good fruit.*
*. . . So by their fruits you will know them.*

—MATTHEW 7:18, 20

God doesn't ask what we believe, or whether we attend
church, or even how we pray. God asks what fruits our
lives are bearing and whether we are willing to share those
fruits with all of God's children.

2 Kings 22:8–13; 23:1–3
Psalm 119
Matthew 7:15–20

# JUNE 28

• ST. IRENAEUS, BISHOP AND MARTYR •

*They have poured out their blood like water*
*round about Jerusalem,*
*and there is no one to bury them.*
*We have become the reproach of our neighbors,*
*the scorn and derision of those around us.*
*O LORD, how long?*
—PSALM 79:3–5

Our news channels flood us with images of the brutality of
conflict and crime. Our entertainment channels overflow
with gratuitous violence. We may consider ourselves
religious (and righteous?); yet other nations strive to
protect themselves from our way of life. Dare we turn, with
the psalmist, to our God and plead, "How long, O Lord?"

2 Kings 24:8–17
Psalm 79
Matthew 7:21–29

⇒ 215 ⇐

*On the very night before Herod was to bring him to trial, Peter, secured by double chains, was sleeping between two soldiers, while outside the door guards kept watch on the prison. Suddenly the angel of the Lord stood by him, and a light shone in the cell. He tapped Peter on the side and awakened him, saying, "Get up quickly." The chains fell from his wrists.*

—ACTS 12:6–7

The angel has to waken Peter by tapping him on the shoulder and urging him to hurry. How wakeful are we to the touch of the angel, which invites us to go beyond the fears that bind us and to let go of the chains that entangle us? The call to freedom demands our response, our wakefulness, and our absolute trust.

| **Vigil:** | **Day:** |
|---|---|
| Acts 3:1–10 | Acts 12:1–11 |
| Psalm 19 | Psalm 34 |
| Galatians 1:11–20 | 2 Timothy 4:6–8, 17–18 |
| John 21:15–19 | Matthew 16:13–19 |

*Rise up, shrill in the night,*
*at the beginning of every watch;*
*Pour out your heart like water*
*in the presence of the Lord;*
*Lift up your hands to him*
*for the lives of your little ones.*
—LAMENTATIONS 2:19

At the darkest hour of the night, a devastated family grieves for a son killed on foreign soil; a lone parent searches the streets for a rebellious teenager; a mother cradles her dying child in the silence of the hospice. God hears their cries and asks us to stretch out our hands in compassion.

Lamentations 2:2, 10–14, 18–19
Psalm 74
Matthew 8:5–17

*For you know the gracious act of our Lord Jesus Christ, that though he was rich, for your sake he became poor, so that by his poverty you might become rich.*

—2 CORINTHIANS 8:9

Authentic loving asks that we empty ourselves to fill one another. Our emptiness then becomes the sacred space into which God pours God's own love and life so that our own reservoir of loving never be exhausted.

Wisdom 1:13–15; 2:23–24
Psalm 30
2 Corinthians 8:7, 9, 13–15
Mark 5:21–43 or 5:21–24, 35–43

*Foxes have dens and birds of the sky have nests,*
*but the Son of Man has nowhere to rest his head.*

—MATTHEW 8:20

In following Jesus, we must be willing to leave every temporary yet comfortable lodging place. When we have nowhere to call home, then everywhere becomes home, because we dwell with the One who calls us beyond all human resting places.

Amos 2:6–10, 13–16
Psalm 50
Matthew 8:18–22

*Tuesday*

# JULY 3

*Jesus said to [Thomas], "Have you come to believe because you have seen me? Blessed are those who have not seen and have believed."*

—JOHN 20:29

Let us ask not for the gift of proof,
but for the grace to trust.

Ephesians 2:19–22
Psalm 117
John 20:24–29

*Away with your noisy songs!*
*I will not listen to the melodies of your harps.*
*But if you would offer me burnt offerings,*
*then let justice surge like water,*
*and goodness like an unfailing stream.*

—AMOS 5:23–24

This world often deafens us with the chanting of its many empty promises. Justice flows only in spoonfuls, and when we encounter goodness, especially in high places, it surprises us. The prophet turns our reality on its head; in the Kingdom, the noice is silenced and all we hear are the rushing waters of justice and goodness.

Amos 5:14–15, 21–24
Psalm 50
Matthew 8:28–34

*The law of the LORD is perfect,*
*refreshing the soul.*
*The decree of the LORD is trustworthy,*
*giving wisdom to the simple.*

—PSALM 19:8

What might revive our flagging spirits in a world held
hostage to the power of the dollar and the bomb?
The psalmist pours three healing words into our wounds:
trust, wisdom, and simplicity—the very nature of God and
the gifts of God's grace.

Amos 7:10–17
Psalm 19
Matthew 9:1–8

*The Pharisees saw this and said to his disciples, "Why does your teacher eat with tax collectors and sinners?" He heard this and said, "Those who are well do not need a physician, but the sick do."*
—MATTHEW 9:11–12

After the Second World War, a Jewish physician, liberated from the camps and barely alive, made his way back to the small Bavarian village that had betrayed him to almost certain death five years earlier. "Why would you go back to the place where you were persecuted?" they asked him. "Because the people need a doctor," he said.

Amos 8:4–6, 9–12
Psalm 119
Matthew 9:9–13

*No one patches an old cloak with a piece of unshrunken cloth, for its fullness pulls away from the cloak and the tear gets worse.*

—MATTHEW 9:16

God's reign is not something we can apply piecemeal to our lives. It is a power that makes us whole by healing us from deep within, cell by cell, thought by thought, and moment by moment. God does not patch old onto the new but makes the old entirely new.

Amos 9:11–15
Psalm 85
Matthew 9:14–17

*My grace is sufficient for you, for power is made perfect in weakness.*
—2 Corinthians 12:9

As long as I try to do things my way, God's power can find no entry to my life. Only when I let go of the struggle and turn to God can the channels of grace flow freely, just as a drowning person may have to be rendered helpless before the lifeguard can carry him to safety.

Ezekiel 2:2–5
Psalm 123
2 Corinthians 12:7–10
Mark 6:1–6

*The LORD is gracious and merciful,
slow to anger and of great kindness.
The LORD is good to all
and compassionate toward all his works.*

—PSALM 145:8–9

The God of compassion, goodness, and love leaves traces of Godself in every area of life, through the spoken words and concrete acts of compassion, love, and goodness we receive from, and offer to, others.

Hosea 2:16–18, 21–22
Psalm 145
Matthew 9:18–26

*At the sight of the crowds, his heart was moved with pity for them*
*because they were troubled and abandoned,*
*like sheep without a shepherd.*

—MATTHEW 9:36

When I am walking down the street or through the
shopping mall, may God give me the grace to see the
crowds around me not with my spirit of impatience and
irritability but through the eyes of Jesus, who sees how
harassed, dejected, and confused they are.

Hosea 8:4–7, 11–13
Psalm 115
Matthew 9:32–38

*As you go, make this proclamation:*
*"The Kingdom of heaven is at hand."*
—MATTHEW 10:7

The kingdom of heaven is never further from us than our next breath; it is not in some foreign realm beyond our earthly reach, but in present experience—in our very cells, our neighbor's face or voice, our every encounter.

Hosea 10:1–3, 7–8, 12
Psalm 105
Matthew 10:1–7

*Yet it was I who taught Ephraim to walk,*
*who took them in my arms;*
*I drew them with human cords,*
*with bands of love.*
*. . . Yet though I stooped to feed my child,*
*they did not know that I was their healer.*

—HOSEA 11:3–4

The reins that my granddaughter sees as restraints and restrictions are actually our way of showing that we love her too much to let her run off into danger. One day she will grow beyond her present frustrations to understand that these are reins of love.

Hosea 11:1–4, 8–9
Psalm 80
Matthew 10:7–15

---

*I will be like the dew for Israel:*
*he shall blossom like the lily;*
*He shall strike root like the Lebanon cedar,*
*and put forth his shoots.*

—HOSEA 14:6–7

The dewdrop that glistens so beautifully at dawn is gone by noon, but it has actually soaked into the parched soil to give life to deep roots. Our glimpses of God can also seem fleeting, but they bring us to life at our core, long after we think they have slipped away into mere memory.

Hosea 14:2–10
Psalm 51
Matthew 10:16–23

*Then I heard the voice of the LORD saying:*
*"Whom shall I send? Who will go for us?"*
*"Here I am," I said; "send me!"*
—ISAIAH 6:8

God asks for volunteers, not conscripts, to take the
message of love and peace to the world.

Isaiah 6:1–8
Psalm 93
Matthew 10:24–33

*He said to them, "Wherever you enter a house, stay there until you leave. Whatever place does not welcome you or listen to you, leave there and shake the dust off your feet in testimony against them."*

—MARK 6:10–11

Wherever we go, may we arrive trustfully and depart gratefully. And if things don't work out as we had hoped, let us simply leave behind, without rancor, whatever needs to be left behind and move on.

Amos 7:12–15
Psalm 85
Ephesians 1:3–14 or Ephesians 1:3–10
Mark 6:7–13

*Cease doing evil; learn to do good.*
*Make justice your aim: redress the wronged,*
*hear the orphan's plea, defend the widow.*

—ISAIAH 1:16–17

Would you give your vote to a political party with a manifesto like the one in this reading?

Would you willingly pay the taxes to make those ideals a reality?

Will you offer yourself as a candidate in your home constituency for the movement of the kingdom?

Isaiah 1:10–17
Psalm 50
Matthew 10:34–11:1

*Take care you remain tranquil and do not fear; let not your courage fail.*

—ISAIAH 7:4

The issues that undermine our inner peace and activate our fears are likely to be the excess baggage that sinks us. Do we have the courage to throw some of it overboard and give our hearts a chance to rise again?

Isaiah 7:1–9
Psalm 48
Matthew 11:20–24

⇒ 234 ⇐

*I give praise to you, Father, Lord of heaven and earth, for although you have hidden these things from the wise and the learned you have revealed them to the childlike.*

—MATTHEW 11:25

Sometimes we obstruct God's wisdom with our human cleverness. Wisdom flows most readily through hearts and minds that have the openness and receptiveness of a child. Better to be empty and open to God than so full of ourselves that there is no space for anything else.

Isaiah 10:5–7, 13–16
Psalm 94
Matthew 11:25–27

*Take my yoke upon you and learn from me, for I am meek and humble of heart; and you will find rest for yourselves. For my yoke is easy, and my burden light.*

—MATTHEW 11:29–30

God's yoke is not an imposition, but an embrace that carries us beyond our laboring solitude to joyful, fruitful companionship and partnership.

Isaiah 26:7–9, 12, 16–19
Psalm 102
Matthew 11:28–30

*My dwelling, like a shepherd's tent,*
*is struck down and borne away from me;*
*You have folded up my life, like a weaver*
*who severs the last thread.*

—ISAIAH 38:12

We are a pilgrim people, called to keep moving from one level of strength to the next, in the One who grants our existence. When we remember this, the pain of loss and parting becomes the labor pain that constantly brings something new to our life.

Isaiah 38:1–6, 7–8, 21–22
Isaiah 38:10–12, 16
Matthew 12:1–8

*Proudly the wicked harass the afflicted,*
*who are caught in the devices the wicked have contrived.*

—PSALM 10:2

When a handful of powermongers hatch the plots of war in the corridors of power, they hand over the world's poorest and most vulnerable people to death and devastation on the killing fields of the earth. Dare we who bear the name of Christ, allow this to continue in our name?

Micah 2:1–5
Psalm 10
Matthew 12:14–21

# JULY 22

*When [Jesus] disembarked and saw the vast crowd, his heart was moved with pity for them, for they were like sheep without a shepherd; and he began to teach them many things.*

—MARK 6:34

When human shepherds betray their flocks, it is time to go deeper, in search of the only shepherd we can trust.

Jeremiah 23:1–6
Psalm 23
Ephesians 2:13–18
Mark 6:30–34

*You have been told, O man, what is good,*
*and what the LORD requires of you:*
*Only to do the right and to love goodness,*
*and to walk humbly with your God.*

—MICAH 6:8

A journalist indefatigably pursues the exposure
of an injustice. A nurse takes time to sit with a distraught
patient. A politician has the grace to say, "I'm sorry.
I made a mistake."

Perhaps there are more people doing what the Lord asks
than we imagine.

Micah 6:1–4, 6–8
Psalm 50
Matthew 12:38–42

*Shepherd your people with your staff,*
*the flock of your inheritance.*
—MICAH 7:14

God leads with a shepherd's crook. Why do human
leaders so often resort to battering rams, machine guns,
and weapons of mass destruction? Let us cease to rule by
threats and start to follow the One who leads us into hope
and promise.

Micah 7:14–15, 18–20
Psalm 85
Matthew 12:46–50

*The mother of the sons of Zebedee approached Jesus with her sons and did him homage, wishing to ask him for something. He said to her, "What do you wish?" She answered him, "Command that these two sons of mine sit, one at your right and the other at your left, in your Kingdom." Jesus said in reply, "You do not know what you are asking. Can you drink the chalice that I am going to drink?"*

—MATTHEW 20:20-22

We believe that, as baptized Christians, a place at the table of the Lord is ours by right. But how would we respond to Jesus' question, "Can you drink the cup that I am going to drink?" When we hold the chalice in our hands, how do our hearts respond to the challenge?

2 Corinthians 4:7–15
Psalm 126
Matthew 20:20–28

• ST. JOACHIM AND ST. ANNE, PARENTS OF THE BLESSED VIRGIN MARY •

*But blessed are your eyes, because they see, and your ears, because they hear. Amen, I say to you, many prophets and righteous people longed to see what you see but did not see it, and to hear what you hear but did not hear it.*

—MATTHEW 13:16–17

We strain to see and hear the mysteries of God, but when they are revealed, in fleeting moments, they take us completely by surprise. They are quietly and freely given by the God who alone can unstop our ears and take the scales from our eyes.

Jeremiah 2:1–3, 7–8, 12–13
Psalm 36
Matthew 13:10–17

*Then the virgins shall make merry and dance,*
*and young men and old as well.*
*I will turn their mourning into joy,*
*I will console and gladden them after their sorrows.*

—JEREMIAH 31:13

Perhaps this promise is not just some distant hope or vague future promise. Perhaps it is already becoming a reality whenever grief turns to gladness, whenever a conflict is justly resolved, whenever a wrong is forgiven, whenever we stretch out our hand to wipe away another's tears.

Jeremiah 3:14–17
Jeremiah 31:10–13
Matthew 13:18–23

*His slaves said to him, "Do you want us to go and pull them up?"*
*He replied, "No, if you pull up the weeds you might uproot the wheat*
*along with them."*

—MATTHEW 13:28–29

Evil often hides under the guise of something good, and
good outcomes sometimes result from selfish intentions.
Only the head gardener is able to distinguish between the
weed and the wheat.

Jeremiah 7:1–11
Psalm 84
Matthew 13:24–30

---

≥ 245 ≤

*Then Jesus took the loaves, gave thanks, and distributed them to those who were reclining, and also as much of the fish as they wanted.*

—JOHN 6:11

The one who multiplied the loaves and fishes can take the most meager offerings of our hearts and hands and turn them into a feast for others.

2 Kings 4:42–44
Psalm 145
Ephesians 4:1–6
John 6:1–15

*The Kingdom of heaven is like yeast that a woman took and mixed with three measures of wheat flour until the whole batch was leavened.*

—MATTHEW 13:33

There is no way that a bit of yeast wanted to lose its identity by mingling in a bowl full of flour, but its self-surrender became the means of making bread for the world. Perhaps if we could let go of some of our fierce individualism, there might be another miracle.

Jeremiah 13:1–11
Deuteronomy 32:18–21
Matthew 13:31–35

*We wait for peace, to no avail;*
*for a time of healing, but terror comes instead.*
*We recognize, O LORD, our wickedness,*
*the guilt of our fathers;*
*that we have sinned against you.*
—JEREMIAH 14:19–20

We pray for peace from the bottom of our unpeaceful
hearts. We campaign against violence with words and
deeds that betray our violent attitudes. We are getting
nowhere, Lord. Our sacred dreams are subverted by our
sin and by the systemic evil in our systems and institutions.
Only you can set us free from these vicious cycles.

Jeremiah 14:17–22
Psalm 79
Matthew 13:36–43

*The Kingdom of heaven is like a treasure buried in a field, which a person finds and hides again, and out of joy goes and sells all that he has and buys that field.*

—MATTHEW 13:44

We might imagine a family selling their home to pay for life-saving medical treatment for a beloved child. We might even imagine something so precious that we would give everything we have to possess it. Jesus invites us to take hold of this amazing truth: such love, such deep desires in ourselves, are but fleeting glimpses of God's overwhelming love and desire for us, and for our well-being.

Jeremiah 15:10, 16–21
Psalm 59
Matthew 13:44–46

---

*I went down to the potter's house and there he was, working at the wheel. Whenever the object of clay which he was making turned out badly in his hand, he tried again, making of the clay another object of whatever sort he pleased.*

—JEREMIAH 18:3–4

I know for sure that the hands of the Potter have reworked my life's "pot" many times. The story of my pot so far helps me trust the Potter's promise that, whatever may go wrong in the future, God will never give up on me, will never stop reshaping me until I am finally the person he longs for me to be.

Jeremiah 18:1–6
Psalm 146
Matthew 13:47–53

*A prophet is not without honor except in his native place and
in his own house.*

—MATTHEW 13:57

We have come to expect God's messages and signs to
come down with thunderbolts or choirs of angels. Yet the
Christ is much more likely to reveal God's Spirit on our
own doorstep, and we will probably dismiss it when that
happens. Let our gaze not be so firmly fixed on heaven that
we despise the Lord of our earth.

Jeremiah 26:1–9
Psalm 69
Matthew 13:54–58

*See, you lowly ones, and be glad;*
*you who seek God, may your hearts revive!*
*For the LORD hears the poor,*
*and his own who are in bonds he spurns not.*

—PSALM 69:33–34

In his powerful book *A Persistent Peace*, the Jesuit priest John
Dear describes a powerful moment when he prayed the
rosary using the links of the chains that bound him, after
he was arrested in New York City during a peace protest.
The Lord surely listens to the prayers of the poor and
the captives, but he enlists our ears to listen, too, and our
hands to respond to what we hear.

Jeremiah 26:11–16, 24
Psalm 69
Matthew 14:1–12

*The whole Israelite community grumbled against Moses and Aaron.
The Israelites said to them, "Would that we had died at the Lord's hand
in the land of Egypt, as we sat by our fleshpots and ate our fill of bread!
But you had to lead us into this desert to make the whole community
die of famine!"*

—EXODUS 16:2–3

Even liberated people can develop selective memory.
We long for freedom but don't like the work and
responsibility that go with it. So, given half a chance,
we slide back into the relative ease of unfreedom and blame
others for our plight.

Exodus 16:2–4, 12–15
Psalm 78
Ephesians 4:17, 20–24
John 6:24–35

*Then a cloud came, casting a shadow over them; from the cloud came a voice, "This is my beloved Son. Listen to him." Suddenly, looking around, they no longer saw anyone but Jesus alone with them.*

—MARK 9:7–8

The old proverb "Every cloud has a silver lining" is sometimes ironically reversed: "Every silver lining has a cloud." Very quickly, it seems, after his friends glimpsed the glory of Jesus, the cloud obscured their vision. But it was a bright cloud, surely—a cloud that reminds us all that we are living in time and not yet in eternity. We know that a bright cloud holds the glory within it, a symbol, like so many clouds in Scripture, of God's presence.

Daniel 7:9–10, 13–14
Psalm 97
2 Peter 1:16–19
Mark 9:2–10

*Tuesday*

# AUGUST 7

*The LORD looked down from his holy height,*
*from heaven he beheld the earth,*
*To hear the groaning of the prisoners,*
*to release those doomed to die.*

—PSALM 102:20–21

You don't get to hear the groans of the prisoners or of
those on death row unless you keep your ear very close to
the ground, put yourself in their shoes, and feel with them
the desolation of their plight. Prison is a terrifying place to
be, an agonizing place, a risky place, but the incarnate One
makes it very clear that this is our calling, and if we dare go
there, we will find him waiting to receive us.

Jeremiah 30:1–2, 12–15, 18–22
Psalm 102
Matthew 14:22–36 or 15:1–2, 10–14

*He who scattered Israel, now gathers them together,*
*he guards them as a shepherd his flock.*

—JEREMIAH 31:10

God's hands scatter us like seeds to the ends of the earth.
God guards and nourishes us as we grow, and God gathers
us in—a harvest from which God will make bread for
the world.

Jeremiah 31:1–7
Jeremiah 31:10–13
Matthew 15:21–28

*I will place my law within them, and write it upon their hearts;*
*I will be their God, and they shall be my people.*

—JEREMIAH 31:33

God plants God's law in our hearts, not our heads. This
law does not compel us to obedience but calls us to
compassion. Once it lodges in our hearts, we can forge a
new relationship between our God and ourselves.

Jeremiah 31:31–34
Psalm 51
Matthew 16:13–23

*Whoever sows sparingly will also reap sparingly, and whoever sows bountifully will also reap bountifully. Each must do as already determined, without sadness or compulsion, for God loves a cheerful giver. Moreover, God is able to make every grace abundant for you so that in all things, always having all you need, you may have an abundance for every good work.*

—2 CORINTHIANS 9:6–8

A beggar sat by the roadside asking passersby for a few grains of rice. One day the emperor rode by. But instead of giving the beggar rice, he asked the beggar to give him some rice instead. The beggar counted out five grains and gave them to the emperor, who thanked him warmly and went on his way. Later, the beggar discovered, that for each grain of rice he had given, the emperor had returned a nugget of gold. "Oh, how I wish I had given the emperor every grain of rice I possessed!"

2 Corinthians 9:6–10
Psalm 112
John 12:24–26

• ST. CLARE, VIRGIN •

*Amen, I say to you, if you have faith the size of a mustard seed, you will say to this mountain, "Move from here to there," and it will move. Nothing will be impossible for you.*

—MATTHEW 17:20

It takes only a bit of yeast to change a bag of flour into a loaf of bread. It takes only a sliver of faith to turn a self-focused life into one that nourishes others.

Habakkuk 1:12–2:4
Psalm 9
Matthew 17:14–20

# AUGUST 12

*Elijah went a day's journey into the desert, until he came to a broom tree and sat beneath it. He prayed for death saying: "This is enough, O LORD! Take my life, for I am no better than my fathers." He lay down and fell asleep under the broom tree, but then an angel touched him and ordered him to get up and eat. Elijah looked and there at his head was a hearth cake and a jug of water.*

—1 KINGS 19:4–6

Who was the angel who touched your life when you were at the end of the line, the one who gave you the encouragement to keep going? It was probably God, disguised as your friend or neighbor. Will you let God disguise Godself as you when a friend needs an angel?

1 Kings 19:4–8
Psalm 34
Ephesians 4:30–5:2
John 6:41–51

*Jesus asked him, "What is your opinion, Simon? From whom do the kings of the earth take tolls or census tax? From their subjects or from foreigners?" When he said, "From foreigners," Jesus said to him, "Then the subjects are exempt."*

—MATTHEW 17:25–26

Secular authority demands: "Pay and obey." God's authority invites: "Receive and respond."

Ezekiel 1:2–5, 24–28
Psalm 148
Matthew 17:22–27

---

*Amen, I say to you, unless you turn and become like children, you will not enter the Kingdom of heaven. Whoever becomes humble like this child is the greatest in the Kingdom of heaven.*

—MATTHEW 18:3–4

There is really only one obstacle when it comes to entering the kingdom of heaven. We have to get over ourselves.

Ezekiel 2:8–3:4
Psalm 119
Matthew 18:1–5, 10, 12–14

• ASSUMPTION OF THE BLESSED VIRGIN MARY •

*My soul proclaims the greatness of the Lord;*
*my spirit rejoices in God my Savior*
*for he has looked with favor on his lowly servant.*
*From this day all generations will call me blessed:*
*the Almighty has done great things for me.*
—LUKE 1:46–48

Two young maidens sat one morning beside a perfectly still
pool of clear water. Each gazed into the pool. One saw her
own reflection and marveled at her beauty. The other saw
the glory of the skies, the fleeting clouds, and the bright
sun, and she gave thanks to God for all creation. Today we
honor the one who demonstrates that true humility can
recognize true greatness.

| Vigil: | Day: |
|---|---|
| 1 Chronicles 15:3–4, 15–16; 16:1–2 | Revelation 11:19; 12:1–6, 10 |
| Psalm 132 | Psalm 45 |
| 1 Corinthians 15:54–57 | 1 Corinthians 15:20–27 |
| Luke 11:27–28 | Luke 1:39–56 |

# AUGUST 16

*Peter approached Jesus and asked him, "Lord, if my brother sins against me, how often must I forgive him? As many as seven times?" Jesus answered, "I say to you, not seven times but seventy-seven times."*

—MATTHEW 18:21–22

Jesus challenges us to change our grudging teaspoons of forgiveness into unstinting expressions of love.

Ezekiel 12:1–12
Psalm 78
Matthew 18:21–19:1

*But you were captivated by your own beauty, you used your renown
to make yourself a harlot, and you lavished your harlotry on every
passer-by, whose own you became. . . .*

*Yet I will remember the covenant I made with you.*
—EZEKIEL 16:15, 60

Have we been carried away by our own delusions of
grandeur? Have we prostituted our principles to the
gods of profit or popularity? Have we compromised our
integrity by selling unprincipled entertainment or weapons
of death to all who come with the means to pay?
God remembers God's covenant with us. But do we?

Ezekiel 16:1–15, 60, 63, or 16:59–63
Isaiah 12:2–6
Matthew 19:3–12

*What is the meaning of this proverb that you recite in the land of Israel:*
*"Fathers have eaten green grapes,*
*thus their children's teeth are on edge"?*
*. . . For I have no pleasure in the death of anyone who dies, says the*
*Lord GOD. Return and live!*
—EZEKIEL 18:1–2, 32

Our children and grandchildren will bear the consequences
of our exploitation of the planet and our unbridled
warmongering. God calls us, with infinite patience, to stop
and think about what we are doing, to choose life and
renounce the strategies of death and destruction—for our
sakes, for God's sake, and for the sake of those still unborn.

Ezekiel 18:1–10, 13, 30–32
Psalm 51
Matthew 19:13–15

*I will bless the LORD at all times;*
*his praise shall be ever in my mouth.*
*Let my soul glory in the LORD;*
*the lowly will hear me and be glad.*
—PSALM 34:2–3

All seeking after and striving for peace in our world begins
in the most unpeaceful place we know: our own hearts.
When we tune in to the heartbeat of God, then our words
will be truthful and our actions pure. Only then will the
world begin to move closer to God's peace.

Proverbs 9:1–6
Psalm 34
Ephesians 5:15–20
John 6:51–58

*All of these [commandments] I have observed. What do I still lack?*
—MATTHEW 19:20

The spiritual journey has been compared to taking a close-up photo of the horizon; however far along we go, there is always more. Jesus invites us, along with the rich young man in the Gospel story, to walk the paths we know to be right and to be alert to "more" that God will reveal to our hearts as we go.

Ezekiel 24:15–23
Deuteronomy 32:18–21
Matthew 19:16–22

# AUGUST 21

• ST. PIUS X, POPE •

*By your great wisdom applied to your trading*
*you have heaped up your riches;*
*your heart has grown haughty from your riches.*
—EZEKIEL 28:5

Money is a seriously addictive substance. There is a very
real danger that the more of it we accumulate, the more
our hearts and souls will shrink. The prophet Ezekiel issues
a timely wake-up call to the world's richest nations.

Ezekiel 28:1–10
Deuteronomy 32:26–28, 30, 35–36
Matthew 19:23–30

*"'Am I not free to do as I wish with my own money? Are you envious because I am generous?' Thus, the last will be first, and the first will be last."*

—MATTHEW 20:15–16

The values of Jesus completely overturn our ideas of fairness and order. Jesus' values call the poorest and most neglected right up to the front of the line. It's a no-lose situation. The first laborers in the vineyard will still receive what they expected, but the last arrivals will be surprised—and elated—at their reward for showing up.

Ezekiel 34:1–11
Psalm 23
Matthew 20:1–16

*I will give you a new heart and place a new spirit within you, taking from your bodies your stony hearts and giving you natural hearts.*
—EZEKIEL 36:26

The prophet promises that our hearts—rock-hard with judgment, criticism, and conflict—can, in God's hands, be transformed into hearts that throb with compassion, love, and care. It begins in the individual heart but will eventually change the world.

Ezekiel 36:23–28
Psalm 51
Matthew 22:1–14

⇒ 271 ⇐

*Jesus saw Nathanael coming toward him and said of him, "Here is a true child of Israel. There is no duplicity in him." Nathanael said to him, "How do you know me?" Jesus answered and said to him, "Before Philip called you, I saw you under the fig tree."*

—JOHN 1:47–48

God knows us for who we truly are and recognizes the quality of our innermost being long before we have any awareness of God's presence. As we go about our daily work, or take our rest in the evening, let us remember that when Jesus passes by, he sees us with God's vision.

Revelation 21:9–14
Psalm 145
John 1:45–51

*I will hear what God proclaims;*
*the LORD—for he proclaims peace*
*to his people.*
*Near indeed is his salvation*
*to those who fear him.*
—PSALM 85:9

To hear the voice that speaks of peace, we first have to call
a halt to the clamor of war. The still, small voice of peace
seeps into our consciousness through the gaps between the
thunderbolts of our aggression, but let us be assured that
God will use every gap!

Ezekiel 43:1–7
Psalm 85
Matthew 23:1–12

---

*But the people answered, "Far be it from us to forsake the Lord for the service of other gods. For it was the Lord, our God, who brought us and our fathers up out of the land of Egypt, out of a state of slavery. He performed those great miracles before our very eyes and protected us along our entire journey and among the peoples through whom we passed."*

—JOSHUA 24:16–17

When we look back over our life's journey and see how God has kept surprising us around every bend in the road, leading us through the hazards, and rejoicing with us in the special moments, how can we choose not to walk forward with our God?

Joshua 24:1–2, 15–18
Psalm 34
Ephesians 5:21–32 or 5:2, 25–32
John 6:60–69

*Jesus said to the crowds and to his disciples: "Woe to you, scribes and Pharisees, you hypocrites. You lock the Kingdom of heaven before men. You do not enter yourselves, nor do you allow entrance to those trying to enter."*

—MATTHEW 23:13

The kingdom of heaven has no locks or bolts.
If you should find a fierce Rottweiler barring the entrance,
don't let it frighten you away. It isn't God's.
God doesn't use watchdogs.

2 Thessalonians 1:1–5, 11–12
Psalm 96
Matthew 23:13–22

*Woe to you, scribes and Pharisees, you hypocrites. You cleanse the outside of cup and dish, but inside they are full of plunder and self-indulgence. Blind Pharisee, cleanse first the inside of the cup, so that the outside also may be clean.*

—MATTHEW 23:25–26

Smooth, enticing talk can come from a heart with dark intentions. But destructive words never come out of a heart that is pure.

2 Thessalonians 2:1–3, 14–17
Psalm 96
Matthew 23:23–26

# AUGUST 29

*Herod feared John, knowing him to be a righteous and holy man, and kept him in custody. When he heard him speak he was very much perplexed, yet he liked to listen to him.*

—MARK 6:20

Herod is revealed in today's Gospel reading as a weak and confused person, fearing John but secretly admiring him, recognizing the truth of his challenge but terrified of its consequences. This lethal cocktail of fear and confusion will turn him into a killer.

2 Thessalonians 3:6–10, 16–18
Psalm 128
Mark 6:17–29

# AUGUST 30

*Stay awake! For you do not know on which day your Lord will come.*
—MATTHEW 24:42

Our state of readiness in the context of personal and
national security is so intense as to verge on paranoia.
How strange that we feel no urgency to ready ourselves
to welcome the coming of God into our lives.

1 Corinthians 1:1–9
Psalm 145
Matthew 24:42–51

*The foolishness of God is wiser than human wisdom,*
*and the weakness of God is stronger than human strength.*

—1 CORINTHIANS 1:25

God finds entrance into our hearts and lives through
the cracks and the weak points. How ironic that we spend
so much energy trying to cover up the cracks and hide
the weaknesses.

1 Corinthians 1:17–25
Psalm 33
Matthew 25:1–13

*Well done, my good and faithful servant. Since you were faithful in small matters, I will give you great responsibilities.*

—MATTHEW 25:23

God starts small. We tend to do the opposite: we have plenty of big ideas and high ideals, but we're not so scrupulous when it comes to life's little details. God invites us to work first on the small and hidden acts of generosity, the word of truth instead of deception, the humility to admit to our family or colleagues that we got things wrong. Then God might lead us to bigger things, like world peace and the elimination of poverty.

1 Corinthians 1:26–31
Psalm 33
Matthew 25:14–30

# SEPTEMBER 2

*Who shall live on your holy mountain, O LORD?*
*Whoever walks blamelessly and does justice;*
*who thinks the truth in his heart*
*and slanders not with his tongue.*

—PSALM 15:1–3

If we are tempted to occupy the moral high ground, let us take careful note of the qualifications for dwelling there: a faultless life expressed in just actions and honest words. This territory is almost deserted; everyone stakes a claim to be there, but no one gets to stay very long.

Deuteronomy 4:1–2, 6–8
Psalm 15
James 1:17–18, 21–22, 27
Mark 7:1–8, 14–15, 21–23

*When the people in the synagogue heard this, they were all filled with fury. They rose up, drove him out of the town, and led him to the brow of the hill on which their town had been built, to hurl him down headlong. But he passed through the midst of them and went away.*

—LUKE 4:28–30

How quickly adulation turns to accusation. The people who had been amazed at Jesus' teaching turned on him as soon as he challenged them, and they tried to run him out of town. Jesus walked away. There is a time to confront and a time to walk away from confrontation. May we have the grace to know the difference.

1 Corinthians 2:1–5
Psalm 119
Luke 4:16–30

# SEPTEMBER 4

*We speak about them not with words taught by human wisdom,
but with words taught by the Spirit, describing spiritual realities in
spiritual terms.*

—1 CORINTHIANS 2:13

The wisdom of the Spirit penetrates our being through
the heart and not the head. It transforms us at the deepest
level, and that transformation changes everything: how we
think, act, and relate to one another and to God.

1 Corinthians 2:10–16
Psalm 145
Luke 4:31–37

*I planted, Apollos watered, but God caused the growth. Therefore, neither the one who plants nor the one who waters is anything, but only God, who causes the growth.*

—1 CORINTHIANS 3:6–7

Growth of heart and spirit can come only from the source of all life and from the divine energy that brings all creation into being. Yet we also have our roles to fulfill in the garden of life, as planters and waterers who coax, nourish, and encourage that life to flourish and bear fruit, in ourselves and in one another.

1 Corinthians 3:1–9
Psalm 33
Luke 4:38–44

*Put out into deep water and lower your nets for a catch.*

—LUKE 5:4

The most unsafe place to be while in a boat is too close
to the land, where we can easily run aground in shallow
water. This is no less true for our life with God. When we
cling to our former securities, we can run aground and get
stuck. If we risk the deeper waters, we may be astounded at
the treasure those depths will yield.

1 Corinthians 3:18–23
Psalm 24
Luke 5:1–11

*Therefore, do not make any judgment before the appointed time, until the Lord comes, for he will bring to light what is hidden in darkness and will manifest the motives of our hearts.*

—1 CORINTHIANS 4:5

I became increasingly irritated with the person sitting next to me on a transatlantic flight. She seemed surly and excessively demanding of the flight attendant. I had her down as a self-centered, grumpy old lady. Then we arrived at Heathrow and I saw that she was utterly lost and frightened. I guided her through the challenges of reaching her connecting flight. She turned to me, face alight with gratitude. "You've been so kind," she said. I wanted to sink into the ground. Thank God she didn't see my premature judgments before God changed them into compassion.

1 Corinthians 4:1–5
Psalm 37
Luke 5:33–39

*Let me sing of the Lord, "He has been good to me."*

—PSALM 13:6

Psalm 13 is a birthday psalm! It begins with the plea to God for an end to the waiting: "How much longer? How much longer? How much longer?" But in its final verse, it reaches this beautiful moment in which the one who pleads becomes the one who sings out for joy. This is the pattern of nearly every pregnancy and birth: an apparently unending, waiting period, then great pain, and then the song of joy at new life. How powerful is this pattern in the birth of the one who will be the mother of the Lord? We rejoice today that the time of waiting becomes, in God's hands, a time for rejoicing.

Micah 5:1–4 or Romans 8:28–30
Psalm 13
Matthew 1:1–16, 18–23 or 1:18–23

*Then will the eyes of the blind be opened,*
*the ears of the deaf be cleared;*
*Then will the lame leap like a stag,*
*then the tongue of the mute will sing.*

—ISAIAH 35:5–6

It's in a prophet's nature to issue wake-up calls. The vocation is still alive and active. Certain people, certain books, and certain defining moments have vividly woken me from my complacency. Scales fell from my eyes. Truth penetrated my understanding. When this happens, we are left with no choice but to speak with our mouths what we know in our hearts.

Isaiah 35:4–7
Psalm 146
James 2:1–5
Mark 7:31–37

*[Jesus said to the man]: "Stretch out your hand." He did so and his hand was restored.*

—LUKE 6:10

Often it is only when we stretch out our hands toward another who needs our help that we are cured of our own paralysis. Self-pity can become compassion, and the suffering patient can become a healer.

1 Corinthians 5:1–8
Psalm 5
Luke 6:6–11

# SEPTEMBER 11

*Jesus departed to the mountain to pray, and he spent the night in prayer to God. When day came, he called his disciples to himself, and from them he chose Twelve.*

—LUKE 6:12–13

Wise choices are born in the silence of prayer. The true direction emerges after we have turned our hearts and minds toward God.

1 Corinthians 6:1–11
Psalm 149
Luke 6:12–19

*Blessed are you who are poor,*
*for the Kingdom of God is yours.*
*Blessed are you who are now hungry,*
*for you will be satisfied.*
*Blessed are you who are now weeping,*
*for you will laugh.*

—LUKE 6:20–21

To recognize the potential for fullness of life that abides in our hearts, we first need to face our inner poverty. To feast on God's love with relish, we first need to feel our aching hunger for it. To embrace our joy, we must first befriend sorrow.

1 Corinthians 7:25–31
Psalm 45
Luke 6:20–26

*Truly you have formed my inmost being;*
*you knit me in my mother's womb.*
*I give you thanks that I am fearfully,*
*wonderfully made; wonderful are your works.*

—PSALM 139:13–14

I never could master the art of knitting, in spite of my mother's best efforts to teach me. It always amazes me to watch someone engaged in that long and infinitely patient work of crafting each stitch to produce a piece of clothing both perfect and unique—and one that will delight another and keep him or her warm. And so God knits each being— gently, patiently, cell by cell—to shape a unique and lovely person who will bring joy and warmth to others.

1 Corinthians 8:1–7, 11–13
Psalm 139
Luke 6:27–38

## Friday

# SEPTEMBER 14

• THE EXALTATION OF THE HOLY CROSS •

*Just as Moses lifted up the serpent in the desert, so must the Son of Man be lifted up, so that everyone who believes in him may have eternal life.*
—JOHN 3:14–15

On the cross of Christ, all our human contradictions and paradoxes are resolved. Brutality intersects with compassion; fear intersects with love. The serpent, a symbol for Jews and Christians of the evil power of temptation and seduction is transformed into the symbol of the healing professions. Many Christians wear a cross as a mark of faith. When we do, can we allow ourselves the awareness of how those contradictions and paradoxes are being resolved in our lives as they hang with Jesus at the place of execution?

Numbers 21:4–9
Psalm 78
Philippians 2:6–11
John 3:13–17

*Jesus' father and mother were amazed at what was said about him; and Simeon blessed them and said to Mary, his mother, "Behold, this child is destined for the fall and rise of many in Israel, and to be a sign that will be contradicted and you yourself a sword will pierce so that the thoughts of many hearts may be revealed."*

—LUKE 2:33–35

When my daughter was a baby, complete strangers would overcome their normal reserve, stop and look at the baby, and wish her well. I felt connected to the whole town at that time, so kind and encouraging people were about the new life I held in my arms. How might it have felt if someone like Simeon had issued a dire warning about everything the baby would become and all the suffering it would entail? Today we remember that Mary was connected to her son's glory and his agony before she had any idea of where all of it would lead.

1 Corinthians 10:14–22
Psalm 31
John 19:25–27 or Luke 2:33–35

*Jesus and his disciples set out for the villages of Caesarea Philippi. Along the way he asked his disciples, "Who do people say that I am?" They said in reply, "John the Baptist, others Elijah, still others one of the prophets." And he asked them, "But who do you say that I am?"*

—MARK 8:27–29

Ask a hundred Christians this question and you will hear a hundred different answers. Take a moment today to hear the question addressed by Jesus to yourself:

Who am I for *you*?

Isaiah 50:5–9
Psalm 116
James 2:14–18
Mark 8:27–35

*I hear that when you meet as a Church there are divisions among you.*
*. . . When you meet in one place, then, it is not to eat the Lord's supper.*

—1 CORINTHIANS 11:18, 20

If we gather at the Lord's table to break the bread
and share the wine but exclude anyone from
participation at that table, let us not presume to call the
gatherings Eucharist.

1 Corinthians 11:17–26, 33
Psalm 40
Luke 7:1–10

# SEPTEMBER 18

*As the body is one though it has many parts and all the parts of the body, though many, are one body, so also Christ.*

—1 CORINTHIANS 12:12

Where do the colors black, brown, and white make a rainbow? In postapartheid South Africa, where every South African, regardless of race or color, became a citizen of what they themselves call the Rainbow Nation. How much more is the Body of Christ called to a rainbow existence in which every searching soul is welcome and God's promises are proclaimed in the midst of our differences.

1 Corinthians 12:12–14, 27–31
Psalm 100
Luke 7:11–17

*So faith, hope, love remain, these three; but the greatest of these is love.*

—1 CORINTHIANS 13:13

Faith teaches us to trust ourselves, one another, and God.

Hope keeps us going, striving always for what makes us more truly human.

But it is love that binds us together and shapes us into communities of life.

1 Corinthians 12:31—13:13
Psalm 33
Luke 7:31—35

[Jesus said]: "*Two people were in debt to a certain creditor; one owed five hundred days' wages and the other owed fifty. Since they were unable to repay the debt, he forgave it for both. Which of them will love him more?*" *Simon said in reply,* "*The one, I suppose, whose larger debt was forgiven.*"

—LUKE 7:41–43

Until I fell sick, I had no appreciation of the many people who dedicate their lives to the care of others. Only in a hospital bed did I learn what gratitude means. Until I lost my way and wandered far from God, I had no appreciation of the depths of God's loving forgiveness. Only in the darkness of sin and failure did I learn what love means.

1 Corinthians 15:1–11
Psalm 118
Luke 7:36–50

---

*The Pharisees saw this and said to his disciples, "Why does your teacher eat with tax collectors and sinners?" He heard this and said, "Those who are well do not need a physician, but the sick do."*

—MATTHEW 9:11–12

We all have our fantasies about what heaven might be like. I smiled once to hear someone comment that when we get to heaven, we might be surprised to find who else is there—people we would have thought had no chance whatever of gaining entrance. But what might surprise us more will be the expression of amazement on their faces, to discover that we have been let in!

Ephesians 4:1–7, 11–13
Psalm 19
Matthew 9:9–13

*A sower went out to sow his seed. And as he sowed, some seed fell on the path and was trampled, and the birds of the sky ate it up. Some seed fell on rocky ground, and when it grew, it withered for lack of moisture. Some seed fell among thorns, and the thorns grew with it and choked it. And some seed fell on good soil, and when it grew, it produced fruit a hundredfold.*

—LUKE 8:5–8

Let us be humbly mindful of the seeds in our lives that have been stunted and left to die. But let us mainly pour our energy, our attention, and our resources into the seeds that are growing in good soil. What we feed will grow. What we starve will shrink. Which seeds do we want to grow?

1 Corinthians 15:35–37, 42–49
Psalm 56
Luke 8:4–15

*Where do the wars and where do the conflicts among you come from?*
*Is it not from your passions that make war within your members? You*
*covet but do not possess. You kill and envy but you cannot obtain; you*
*fight and wage war.*

—JAMES 4:1–2

It is said that in a democracy we get the government we deserve. It follows that our nations' foreign policies reflect the state of our own hearts. God of all peace, give us the grace to recognize that the world's killing fields have their root in our personal anger, violence, and greed and to seek your peace within us, so that we might bring peace to the larger world.

Wisdom 2:12, 17–20
Psalm 54
James 3:16–4:3
Mark 9:30–37

*There is nothing hidden that will not become visible, and nothing secret that will not be known and come to light.*

—LUKE 8:17

We may fear the searchlight that exposes all our darkest corners. But the same beam of love brings to light hidden gifts as well, and blessings that we never guessed we had.

Proverbs 3:27–34
Psalm 15
Luke 8:16–18

# SEPTEMBER 25

*My mother and my brothers are those who hear the word of God
and act on it.*

—LUKE 8:21

Perhaps God isn't so interested in what we believe, but in
how we live, not in the doctrines we have absorbed but in
what we do, what we say, and how we live in our streets
and homes and communities. Surely, at the end of the road,
we will not be asked: "Can you say the creed?" but rather
"Have you added a bit of love into the world?"

Proverbs 21:1–6, 10–13
Psalm 119
Luke 8:19–21

# SEPTEMBER 26

*Give me neither poverty nor riches;*
*provide me only with the food I need;*
*Lest, being full, I deny you,*
*saying, "Who is the LORD?"*
—PROVERBS 30:8–9

The word *enough* has lost its meaning in affluent Western
societies. If we have too little, we can become totally
absorbed in the need to survive. If we have too much, we
can start to believe in the illusion of our self-sufficiency.
Enough is probably more than we need and much less
than we want. It satisfies us but keeps us mindful of
our dependence on God. Best of all, having enough for
ourselves leaves plenty to spare so that others, too,
can have enough.

Proverbs 30:5–9
Psalm 119
Luke 9:1–6

# SEPTEMBER 27

• ST. VINCENT DE PAUL, PRIEST •

*Teach us to number our days aright,*
*that we may gain wisdom of heart.*
—PSALM 90:12

Nothing focuses our minds so sharply on what we have as the imminent possibility of losing it. Terminal illness can reveal, perhaps for the first time, just how precious the gift of life is. The loss of a loved one reveals, agonizingly, just how much that person means to us. Perhaps we live each day most fully when we live it as if it were our last.

Ecclesiastes 1:2–11
Psalm 90
Luke 9:7–9

*There is an appointed time for everything,*
*and a time for every thing under the heavens.*
—ECCLESIASTES 3:1

As the leaves are falling and small creatures are preparing
for hibernation in the exposed wilds of Scotland, so, too,
are the Atlantic salmon struggling upstream to lay their
eggs in the waters where they began their lives, four years
earlier. In death, new life is launched, and the seasons of
living and dying weave their pattern through our lives, too.
There is a time to leap to life and a time to let go of life.
We are wise when we recognize the seasons of our soul
and live into them.

Ecclesiastes 3:1–11
Psalm 144
Luke 9:18–22

*Amen, amen, I say to you, you will see heaven opened and the angels of God ascending and descending on the Son of Man.*

—JOHN 1:51

I lived for three years in West Berlin, at the height of the Cold War. The city was artificially severed from its hinterland, and we lived disconnected from all that lay around us. Then the Berlin Wall came down, and we could visit those places that had been only names on a map. The people reconnected with their natural geographical state. Today we catch a glimpse of what our natural spiritual state is like. It is a place of unbroken connections where the angels ascend and descend constantly, holding heaven and earth together in God's infinite love and keeping the channels of connection open until we shall see things as they really are.

Daniel 7:9–10, 13–14, or Revelation 12:7–12
Psalm 138
John 1:47–51

*If your hand causes you to sin, cut it off. It is better for you to enter
into life maimed than with two hands to go into Gehenna.*

—MARK 9:43

Most of us would not hesitate to consent to the removal of
diseased tissue from our bodies, if it was compromising our
health. Why, then, do we cling so ferociously to attitudes
and habits that are not, or are not longer, leading us closer
to our true destiny in God but are instead compromising
our spiritual health and wholeness?

Numbers 11:25–29
Psalm 19
James 5:1–6
Mark 9:38–43, 45, 47–48

*The one who is least among all of you is the one who is the greatest.*

—LUKE 9:48

When I am full of myself, there is no room for God. The less there is of me, the more there is of God-in-me and the more I become my true self in God.

Job 1:6–22
Psalm 17
Luke 9:46–50

—————————————

# OCTOBER 2

• THE HOLY GUARDIAN ANGELS •

*See that you do not despise one of these little ones, for I say to you that their angels in heaven always look upon the face of my heavenly Father.*
—MATTHEW 18:10

There's a well-known story of a three-year-old whose first words to her new baby brother were: "Please tell me about God—I'm beginning to forget."

Job 3:1–3, 11–17, 20–23
Psalm 88
Matthew 18:1–5, 10

*No one who sets a hand to the plow and looks to what was left behind
is fit for the Kingdom of God.*

—LUKE 9:62

The crop will not grow in a field when the plowman has
given up and gone home. The harvest of God's reign will
not come to fullness if we, the laborers, give up on the
challenges of justice, peace, and love. The life of the Spirit
calls us in one direction only: forward.

Job 9:1–12, 14–16
Psalm 88
Luke 9:57–62

*I believe that I shall see the bounty of the LORD*
*in the land of the living.*
*Wait for the LORD with courage; be stouthearted,*
*and wait for the LORD.*
—PSALM 27:13–14

Hope feeds on those moments in which we catch glimpses of God's goodness right here, in the land of the living. They come in the shape of an encouraging word, an act of kindness, a generous gesture. They keep us hoping through apparently hopeless situations, and they strengthen us into people of faith.

Job 19:21–27
Psalm 27
Luke 10:1–12

⇒ 313 ⇐

*Truly you have formed my inmost being;*
*you knit me in my mother's womb.*
*I give you thanks that I am fearfully, wonderfully made;*
*wonderful are your works.*

—PSALM 139:13–14

You are a handcrafted labor of love. There never was, and never will be, another you. God rejoices every moment at this stupendous truth. Do you?

Job 38:1, 12–21; 40:3–5
Psalm 139
Luke 10:13–16

# OCTOBER 6

*At that very moment he rejoiced in the Holy Spirit and said,
"I give you praise, Father, Lord of heaven and earth, for although you
have hidden these things from the wise and the learned you have revealed
them to the childlike."*

—LUKE 10:21

A child sees the wonder of life in every beetle and flower.
The more we learn, the more our vision narrows until
wonder and innocence are lost to achievement
and sophistication.

Job 42:1–3, 5–6, 12–17
Psalm 119
Luke 10:17–24

---

*Let the children come to me; do not prevent them, for the kingdom of God belongs to such as these. Amen, I say to you, whoever does not accept the kingdom of God like a child will not enter it.*

—MARK 10:14–15

A little child is a discoverer, not a conqueror; an explorer, not a controller; a wonderer, not a possessor. May we have the grace to approach God with the heart of a child, by desiring to encounter the mystery and not to contain it.

Genesis 2:18–24
Psalm 128
Hebrews 2:9–11
Mark 10:2–16 or 10:2–12

*The works of his hands are faithful and just;*
*sure are all his precepts.*
*Reliable forever and ever,*
*wrought in truth and equity.*
—PSALM 111:7–8

I drove out of town, gratefully leaving behind the frenzied pace of urban living. I headed west to the mountains. At first the Rockies were a distant, beckoning presence. But the closer I came, the more they enfolded me in their timeless, unchanging strength and solidity. It was a graced day, a life-giving journey, and I can repeat it any time, just by stepping into the quiet space of the heart and allowing myself to be enfolded in God's changeless love.

Galatians 1:6–12
Psalm 111
Luke 10:25–37

*Martha, Martha, you are anxious and worried about many things.*
*There is need of only one thing. Mary has chosen the better part and it*
*will not be taken from her.*

—LUKE 10:41–42

All day I run rings around myself trying to juggle all the
things I have convinced myself that I need to do. May I
have the grace, when night falls, to follow my inner Mary
into the still center where only one thing matters: to know
myself held by God, who steadies my busyness into a
blessed calm.

Galatians 1:13–24
Psalm 139
Luke 10:38–42

*Forgive us our sins
for we ourselves forgive everyone in debt to us.*
—LUKE 11:4

The two parts of this line of prayer are eternally and
inseparably joined. We cannot ask forgiveness from God
or from one another without committing ourselves to be
people who forgive others. The gift of forgiveness is a gift
that we cannot hold on to but must always pass on. Is there
someone who is waiting, today, to receive the forgiveness
from you that you have received from God?

Galatians 2:1–2, 7–14
Psalm 117
Luke 11:1–4

*Are you so stupid? After beginning with the Spirit, are you now ending with the flesh?*

—GALATIANS 3:3

There's a story of an ancient people who discovered a spring of fresh, clear water on the hillside beyond their village. To mark the spot where the water was flowing, the tribe's chief placed a stone at the location of the spring. The people were so delighted with the spring that every time they passed it, they stopped to give thanks and placed another stone beside it. Soon this became a tradition and as time passed many people came to pay homage to the spring and place a stone there, until the flow of water was completely blocked and all that was left was a mountain of ritual stones.

Galatians 3:1–5
Luke 1:69–75
Luke 11:5–13

# OCTOBER 12

*Scripture, which saw in advance that God would justify the Gentiles by faith, foretold the good news to Abraham, saying, "Through you shall all the nations be blessed." Consequently, those who have faith are blessed along with Abraham who had faith.*

—GALATIANS 3:8–9

Paul reminds us that God is, and always was, an ecumenist—welcoming all, whether pagans or Jews, who come with trust in their hearts and who believe in the good news of God's promise. May we have the grace to honor, and to continue, the open welcome of our loving God to all who come in faith.

Galatians 3:7–14
Psalm 111
Luke 11:15–26

*There is neither Jew nor Greek, there is neither slave nor free person,
there is not male and female; for you are all one in Christ Jesus.*

—GALATIANS 3:28

To those whom the One God—the God who holds all in
unity and love—has joined together, let not our man-made
customs and institutions tear us asunder. May all who are
one in Christ Jesus be equally at home in the church that
claims to be his family.

Galatians 3:22–29
Psalm 105
Luke 11:27–28

*Indeed the word of God is living and effective, sharper than any two-edged sword, penetrating even between soul and spirit, joints and marrow, and able to discern reflections and thoughts of the heart.*

—HEBREWS 4:12

If Paul had been writing in the twenty-first century, he might have compared the word of God to a laser beam. In the surgeon's hand, the laser cuts, cauterizes, and heals. It restores sight and destroys what is hostile to life. My own laser flashlight guides me home in the dark, seeking the way past all the obstacles and lighting up the keyhole that opens the door to home. How much more powerful than all of these things is God's word!

Wisdom 7:7–11
Psalm 90
Hebrews 4:12–13
Mark 10:17–30 or 10:17–27

*For freedom Christ has set us free; so stand firm and do not submit again to the yoke of slavery.*

—GALATIANS 5:1

How blind we are, we who fight for our political freedoms and then sell ourselves to the slavery of the marketplace. From the midst of our compulsions and addictions, how little we understand of freedom, and how desperately we need to hear, anew every day, the good news of the deep liberation that Christ has opened up for us.

Galatians 4:22–24, 26–27, 31–5:1
Psalm 113
Luke 11:29–32

*Oh you Pharisees! Although you cleanse the outside of the cup and the dish, inside you are filled with plunder and evil.*

—LUKE 11:39

The gospel message turns each of us inside out. What is revealed on the inside may look very different from the image we present on the outside. How easy it is to see this disconnection in others; how hard to recognize it in ourselves.

Galatians 5:1–6
Psalm 119
Luke 11:37–41

---

⇒ 325 ⇐

*The fruit of the Spirit is love, joy, peace, patience, kindness, generosity,*
*faithfulness, gentleness, self-control.*

—GALATIANS 5:22

It is interesting to note some of the things that are not
the fruits of the Spirit: fear, judgment, division, exclusion,
suspicion, and secrecy. Whenever and wherever we
encounter these things, we can be sure that the
Spirit is not in them.

Galatians 5:18–25
Psalm 1
Luke 11:42–46

*Whatever town you enter and they welcome you, eat what is set before you, cure the sick in it and say to them, "The Kingdom of God is at hand for you."*

—LUKE 10:8–9

Most of us are not itinerant evangelists like Luke, but the guidelines still apply. We are urged, in our normal dealings with one another, to observe simple rules: to share table fellowship as a mark of friendship and trust; to let our presence in any situation be an influence for healing and well-being; and to speak of our faith in terms of our own experience of God's power in our life so that others may realize that God is indeed close by, and in fact right there with them.

2 Timothy 4:10–17
Psalm 145
Luke 10:1–9

• ST. JOHN DE BRÉBEUF AND ST. ISAAC JOGUES, PRIESTS AND MARTYRS,
AND THEIR COMPANIONS, MARTYRS •

*There is nothing concealed that will not be revealed, nor secret that will not be known. Therefore whatever you have said in the darkness will be heard in the light.*

—LUKE 12:2–3

Our minds are like darkened rooms, where no one can really see what we are thinking and feeling. Imagine, then, when God kindles the light of grace. Are we ready for that?

Ephesians 1:11–14
Psalm 33
Luke 12:1–7

*May the eyes of your hearts be enlightened, that you may know what is the hope that belongs to his call.*

—EPHESIANS 1:18

The same light of grace that we may dread is the very light that reveals so much more than our deceptions and dissembling. The light reveals the fullness of God's promise, and it regenerates our hope and faith and love.

Ephesians 1:15–23
Psalm 8
Luke 12:8–12

*Can you drink the cup that I drink or be baptized with the baptism with which I am baptized?*

—MARK 10:38

If we merely worship Jesus from a distance, however piously and reverently, we will never share his cup or walk his path. If we respond to his invitation to be his companions, we will inevitably share one cup, one road, and one immersion into the agony and ecstasy of grace. It's much easier to worship than to follow.

Isaiah 53:10–11
Psalm 33
Hebrews 4:14–16
Mark 10:35–45 or 10:42–45

*We are his handiwork, created in Christ Jesus for good works that God
has prepared in advance, that we should live in them.*

—EPHESIANS 2:9–10

A true work of art is much more than an image; it holds,
and expresses, something of the deepest heart and soul
of the artist. It can never be duplicated. It invites all who
behold it to enter the mystery and meaning of the one who
created it. What a responsibility! What an amazing reality!

Ephesians 2:1–10
Psalm 100
Luke 12:13–21

*So then you are no longer strangers and sojourners, but you are fellow
citizens with the holy ones and members of the household of God.*

—EPHESIANS 2:19

You are part of God's household—a family member, not
a guest or a stranger. If any religious organization asks
you to produce an entry visa, you will know that you have
come to the wrong place.

Ephesians 2:12–22
Psalm 85
Luke 12:35–38

*Much will be required of the person entrusted with much, and still more
will be demanded of the person entrusted with more.*

—LUKE 12:48

Our beautiful planet, and every creature, every tree,
every flower that lives on it, has been given to us on trust.
Can we hope to return all this to God, through future
generations, having helped it to be fruitful? Can we hope
to return it to God and to future generations at all?

Ephesians 3:2–12
Isaiah 12:2–6
Luke 12:39–48

*[May] he . . . grant you in accord with the riches of his glory to be strengthened with power through his Spirit in the inner self, and that Christ may dwell in your hearts through faith.*

—EPHESIANS 3:16–17

I spend a great deal of effort and energy trying to make my outward and visible self grow strong and healthy. What do I do to open my hidden self to the touch of God's Spirit, so that it can grow to fullness and fruitfulness?

Ephesians 3:14–21
Psalm 33
Luke 12:49–53

# OCTOBER 26

*[There is] one Lord, one faith, one baptism; one God and Father of all,*
*who is over all and through all and in all.*
—EPHESIANS 4:5–6

My mother used to do fine embroidery work. I often watched her select silks from an array of many colors and shades for her many different stitching techniques. After all her toil, a truly beautiful design emerged. She had held the whole design in her mind all along. I saw it only when it was complete. This comes to mind when I think of how God is constantly weaving a divine wholeness and unity from what seems so separate and fragmented.

Ephesians 4:1–6
Psalm 24
Luke 12:54–59

*"For three years now I have come in search of fruit on this fig tree but have found none. So cut it down. Why should it exhaust the soil?" He said in reply, "Sir, leave it for this year also, and I shall cultivate the ground around it and fertilize it; it may bear fruit in the future."*

—LUKE 13:7–9

I cherish a little prayer card my small daughter once gave me as a peace offering following some misdemeanor on her part. It reads: "Please be patient. God hasn't finished with me yet!" I hope and pray that God hasn't finished with me either and that there will be time for digging and fertilizing so that the fruit will grow and mature.

Ephesians 4:7–16
Psalm 122
Luke 13:1–9

*Behold, I will bring them back*
*from the land of the north;*
*I will gather them from the ends of the world.*
—JEREMIAH 31:8

The root of the word *religion* means "to bind together."
Let us work with, and not against, God in this great task of
welcoming and gathering people in.

Jeremiah 31:7–9
Psalm 126
Hebrews 5:1–6
Mark 10:46–52

# OCTOBER 29

*Jesus was teaching in a synagogue on the sabbath. And a woman was there who for eighteen years had been crippled by a spirit; she was bent over, completely incapable of standing erect. When Jesus saw her, he called to her and said, "Woman, you are set free of your infirmity." He laid his hands on her, and she at once stood up straight and glorified God.*

—LUKE 13:10–13

In today's churches, Jesus would find many women and men enfeebled and disempowered by their circumstances and by the abuse of power. He has no hands now but ours with which to touch their lives and hearts and empower them once more to stand straight and reach their full height in the presence and power of their God.

Ephesians 4:32–5:8
Psalm 1
Luke 13:10–17

*To what shall I compare the Kingdom of God? It is like yeast that a woman took and mixed in with three measures of wheat flour until the whole batch of dough was leavened.*

—LUKE 13:20–21

Without yeast, the dough will not rise and there will be no bread. But the yeast cannot work its magic until, and unless, it disintegrates and disperses throughout the flour.

It has to lose itself to become something greater than itself. Only then can the silent power of growth and life be released to become bread for the world.

Ephesians 3:21–33 or 5:2, 25–32
Psalm 128
Luke 13:18–21

*Strive to enter through the narrow gate, for many, I tell you, will attempt to enter but will not be strong enough.*

—LUKE 13:24

The first narrow door each of us must enter is the birth canal, which leads away from the perfect comfort zone of our mother's womb. If we could have perceived our feelings at the point of birth, they would surely have been about fear of the unknown. As we grow and mature there are many other narrow doors that challenge us to risk the unknown territory and to travel by faith. The final narrow door opens up to a reality of which our earthbound minds cannot conceive. But every narrow door is an invitation to trust, to grow, and to journey from certainty to mystery. God will wait patiently until our hearts can answer, "Yes!"

Ephesians 6:1–9
Psalm 145
Luke 13:20–30

*The LORD's are the earth and its fullness;*
*the world and those who dwell in it.*
*For he founded it upon the seas*
*and established it upon the rivers.*

—PSALM 24:1–2

Just imagine if we could envision the world and all creation
as a sacred manifestation of God's love, and every human
being a child of that God, utterly beloved by the Creator.
What might I do or say to nudge that dream further along?
What choices might I make today to help move all of
God's people a little closer to becoming God's saints?

Revelation 7:2–4, 9–14
Psalm 24
1 John 3:1–3
Matthew 5:1–12

• THE COMMEMORATION OF ALL THE FAITHFUL DEPARTED
(ALL SOULS' DAY) •

*Even though I walk in the dark valley*
*I fear no evil; for you are at my side*
*with your rod and your staff*
*that give me courage.*

—PSALM 23:4

When we grieve the loss of those we love, our hearts are
overshadowed by mountains of sorrow, loneliness, anger,
regret, or recrimination. The valley path is dark indeed.
The psalmist doesn't promise us a blaze of light, or that
the valley journey will end early, but he promises us a
companion along—comforting our sorrow; accompanying
our pain; feeling and sharing our loss; and leading us to
where, in time, the clouds will disperse.

Wisdom 3:1–9
Psalm 23
Romans 5:5–11
John 6:37–40

# NOVEMBER 3

*My soul is thirsting for the living God.*
*As the hind longs for the running waters,*
*so my soul longs for you,*
*O God.*

—PSALM 42:1

I never really knew what thirst was until I found myself in the arid heat of Middle Eastern deserts or the equatorial rain forests of Southeast Asia. Perhaps my soul's longing for God reveals itself only when I am lost in my inner deserts or when my spirit is lost in its jungles and mazes. Reach out to us, our God, in our longing, when our longing feels powerless to reach out to you.

Philippians 1:18–26
Psalm 42
Luke 14:1, 7–11

*Hear, O Israel! The LORD is our God, the LORD alone! Therefore, you shall love the LORD, your God, with all your heart, and with all your soul, and with all your strength. Take to heart these words which I enjoin on you today.*

—DEUTERONOMY 6:4–6

All the power in my home or place of work depends ultimately and absolutely on the power of the sun. All the relationships in my life—the love I have for my children, family, and friends—depend just as surely and absolutely on the love of God, without which nothing has life or meaning.

Deuteronomy 6:2–6
Psalm 18
Hebrews 7:23–28
Mark 12:28–34

---

⋗ 344 ⋖

*I have stilled and quieted*
*my soul like a weaned child.*
*Like a weaned child on it mother's lap,*
*so is my soul within me.*
—PSALM 131:2

My spirit is always, and only, at home when it rests in
God's presence, like a trusting baby. But my mind is more
like a wayward toddler, always wanting to take off on its
own adventures, sometimes straying far from home and
often into danger. Yet the One who dreamed me into
existence holds both my mind and my soul in harmony and
love, and constantly calls me home to that center of peace.

Philippians 2:1–4
Psalm 131
Luke 14:12–14

# NOVEMBER 6

*Have among yourselves the same attitude that is also yours in Christ Jesus,*
*Who, though he was in the form of God,*
*did not regard equality with God something to be grasped.*
*Rather, he emptied himself,*
*taking the form of a slave,*
*coming in human likeness.*
—PHILIPPIANS 2:5–7

To be the same as Jesus may seem to be too far beyond
our reach. But we can make a start by emptying ourselves
in small ways. We empty ourselves for others whenever
we give away a free evening to be with someone in need;
whenever we pour out our energy to help a neighbor;
whenever we put our own agenda aside, to listen with love,
as a stranger tells her story.

Philippians 2:5–11
Psalm 22
Luke 14:15–24

*Whoever does not carry his own cross and come after me cannot
be my disciple.*

—LUKE 14:27

To follow Jesus demands that we make our life's choices,
big and small, in the truth and integrity that he incarnates.
To live in his truth will always provoke opposition from all
that is untrue. That opposition will rise up against us, in
small ways or large, and place a cross on our shoulders.

Philippians 2:12–18
Psalm 27
Luke 14:25–33

*What woman having ten coins and losing one would not light a lamp and sweep the house, searching carefully until she finds it? And when she does find it, she calls together her friends and neighbors and says to them, "Rejoice with me because I have found the coin that I lost."*

—LUKE 15:8–9

What we lack, or have lost, always seems more precious to us than what we possess. Perhaps this reflects a spiritual reality, too. No matter how much we acquire of material things, our hearts remain in a state of restless longing for an indefinable "more." And paradoxically, in our loss and emptiness, there is at last space for God to enter and fill the space that no other can satisfy.

Philippians 3:3–8
Psalm 105
Luke 15:1–10

*You are God's building. . . . No one can lay a foundation other than
the one that is there, namely, Jesus Christ.*

—1 CORINTHIANS 3:9

No church, however splendid, can call itself *the* church,
because the church is a people, a pilgrim people, a people
being built up, generation after generation, into God's
people. Each of us is a unique part of this great enterprise,
and it doesn't matter whether we are important or
insignificant in the world's eyes, rich or poor, educated or
untaught.

Ezekiel 47:1–2, 8–9, 12
Psalm 46
1 Corinthians 3:9–11, 16–17
John 2:13–22

*I have learned, in whatever situation I find myself, to be self-sufficient. I know indeed how to live in humble circumstances; I know also how to live with abundance.*

—PHILIPPIANS 4:12

To be content and at balance with how things are, at any given moment, is the first step toward spiritual freedom. It is the freedom to choose the more Christlike, the more loving, the more life-giving course of action, without being swayed by any hope of gain or fear of loss.

Philippians 4:10–19
Psalm 112
Luke 16:9–15

*She left and did as Elijah had said. She was able to eat for a year, and he and her son as well; the jar of flour did not go empty, nor the jug of oil run dry, as the LORD had foretold through Elijah.*

—1 KINGS 17:15–16

Do we have the courage to trust the Lord's promise that if we freely give of ourselves, the supply will be constantly replenished from its true source? What we think is just a trickle of goodness and love in our souls can become an infinite cascade of love pouring from God's heart.

1 Kings 17:10–16
Psalm 146
Hebrews 9:24–28
Mark 12:38–44 or 12:41–44

*Things that cause sin will inevitably occur, but woe to the one through*
*whom they occur. It would be better for him if a millstone were put*
*around his neck and he be thrown into the sea than for him to cause one*
*of these little ones to sin. Be on your guard!*

—LUKE 17:1–3

Sometimes our hearts feel like millstones and life is like an
unending series of blocks and obstacles. What will we do
with those obstacles? They can become another stumbling
block along the way, hindering our path and that of others,
or, in God's grace, they can become stepping-stones,
opening up rather than closing down the way ahead.

Titus 1:1–9
Psalm 24
Luke 17:1–6

*Turn from evil and do good,*
*that you may abide forever.*

—PSALM 37:27

Our heart knows only one home: the dwelling place within
God. Every time we choose a course of action that is not
in tune with the heartbeat of God, we stray a little further
from our true home. Every time we choose the more loving
course of action, we take another step along the road that
leads us home.

Titus 2:1–8, 11–14
Psalm 37
Luke 17:7–10

⩾ 353 ⩽

*And one of them, realizing he had been healed, returned, glorifying God in a loud voice; and he fell at the feet of Jesus and thanked him. He was a Samaritan. Jesus said in reply, "Ten were cleansed, were they not? Where are the other nine? Has none but this foreigner returned to give thanks to God?"*

—LUKE 17:15–18

A good friend of mine was dying of cancer. As he passed through the final months of his life, he told me that his prayer became more and more simple until the only thing he wanted, or needed, to say to God, was "Thank you!" Thank you for all that has been. And thank you for the promise of everything still to be revealed.

Titus 3:1–7
Psalm 23
Luke 17:11–19

*The coming of the Kingdom of God cannot be observed, and no one will announce, "Look, here it is," or, "There it is." For behold, the Kingdom of God is among you.*

—LUKE 17:20–21

Imagine a bowl of dough that rises and grows into a loaf of bread that can feed many. The dough might ask, "Where is that mystery that makes me rise? Where is the yeast?" And the answer would surely be, "No one can point to any part of you and say 'here' or 'there,' because the yeast that makes you rise is in the midst of you, invisibly carrying out its mission to transform you."

Philemon 7–20
Psalm 146
Luke 17:20–25

*Remember the wife of Lot. Whoever seeks to preserve his life will lose it,*
*but whoever loses it will save it.*

—LUKE 17:32–33

When I dwell on the things of the past, I may also turn to
salt and become paralyzed by corrosive resentments. The
things I cling to may become so heavy on my heart that
they rob me of the freedom to move on—to safety and
toward transformation.

2 John 4–9
Psalm 119
Luke 17:26–37

*Well for the man who is gracious and lends,*
*who conducts his affairs with justice;*
*He shall never be moved;*
*the just man shall be in everlasting remembrance.*
—PSALM 112:5–6

Again and again, we are warned that it is right action, not right belief, that reveals our morality. The psalmist reminds us that those who act with compassion and generosity are those who are close to God, whatever their belief system may be. Take time to reflect on your friends and neighbors. Where do you see goodness? Wherever you find it, thank God for it, and let it inspire you.

3 John 5–8
Psalm 112
Luke 18:1–8

---

# NOVEMBER 18

*But the wise shall shine brightly*
*like the splendor of the firmament,*
*and those who lead the many to justice*
*shall be like the stars forever.*

—DANIEL 12:3

The stars in heaven may not have looked like stars on earth. Perhaps they were people like the humble grade-school teacher who gently guided children in the ways of goodness and truth, or perhaps they were grandparents who took time to engage with their grandchildren and tell them the timeless stories of wisdom that we all need to hear. When we enter eternity we may discover that some of its stars have familiar faces.

Daniel 12:1–3
Psalm 16
Hebrews 10:11–14, 18
Mark 13:24–32

# NOVEMBER 19

*[The blind man] shouted, "Jesus, Son of David, have pity on me!" The people walking in front rebuked him, telling him to be silent, but he kept calling out all the more, "Son of David, have pity on me!"*

—LUKE 18:38–39

A cry from the heart judgmental crowds cannot silence or suppress.

A cry from the heart Jesus hears and responds to.

Cries from the heart rise up all around us, every day. Will we try to silence or suppress them? Or will we hear them and, with God's grace, try to respond to them?

Revelation 1:1–4; 2:1–5
Psalm 1
Luke 18:35–43

# NOVEMBER 20

*Behold, I stand at the door and knock. If anyone hears my voice and opens the door, then I will enter his house and dine with him, and he with me. I will give the victor the right to sit with me on my throne.*

—REVELATION 3:20–21

God never comes into our space without an invitation. How often do we invite God to be among us at our meals, whether the modest daily meals eaten in haste and with distraction or the family meals at the holidays? And when God accepts our invitation, God sits not at the head of the table but beside us.

Revelation 3:1–6, 14–22
Psalm 15
Luke 19:1–10

*To everyone who has more will be given, but from the one who has not,
even what he has will be taken away.*

—LUKE 19:26

It seems that when a project is truly inspired by the Spirit,
the fruits will far outweigh the effort we put into it, but if
a project is something we are trying to bring about with
our inadequate strength, the fruits will be minimal in spite
of our efforts. So perhaps we could say this: to everything
that flows with the Spirit, there will be disproportionate
growth; to all that does not truly flow from the Spirit, even
the effort we can bring will come to nothing.

Revelation 4:1–11
Psalm 150
Luke 19:11–28

# NOVEMBER 22

*As Jesus drew near Jerusalem, he saw the city and wept over it, saying,
"If this day you only knew what makes for peace—but now it is hidden
from your eyes. For the days are coming upon you when your enemies
will raise a palisade against you; they will encircle you and hem you
in on all sides. They will smash you to the ground and your children
within you, and they will not leave one stone upon another within you
because you did not recognize the time of your visitation."*

—LUKE 19:41–44

There are defining moments in our personal and national
stories when the gates that lead to understanding and
authentic growth stand open. We rarely recognize them.
We turn back, instead, to the ways of retaliation and
revenge, and a whole spate of destruction follows.

Revelation 5:1–10
Psalm 149
Luke 19:41–44

———————————

*And every day he was teaching in the temple area. The chief priests,
the scribes, and the leaders of the people, meanwhile, were seeking to put
him to death, but they could find no way to accomplish their purpose
because all the people were hanging on his words.*

—LUKE 19:47–48

For every individual who plans for war, there are a million
hearts who long for peace. If enough of these millions
stand up for truth, peace, and justice and follow where the
path of peace leads them, then the forces of destruction
will have no chance of prevailing.

Revelation 10:8–11
Psalm 119
Luke 19:45–48

# NOVEMBER 24

*O God, I will sing a new song to you;*
*With a ten-stringed lyre I will chant your praise.*

—PSALM 144:9

Two caterpillars are chewing their way through the leaves when a butterfly flies over them. One caterpillar says to the other, "You'll never get me up in one of those things." The truth is that not only are we all going up in one of those things but also are actually becoming one of those things. God is hatching a new song in our hearts even while we are still caterpillars, and one day the butterfly gestating within us will fly free and dance to the music of the ten-stringed lyre.

Revelation 11:4–12
Psalm 144
Luke 20:27–40

*"I am the Alpha and the Omega," says the Lord God, "the one who is
and who was and who is to come, the almighty."*

—REVELATION 1:8

We who live along the twisting, winding lines leading
from birth to death often find it hard to see that every
ending is a new beginning. The One who is Lord of time
and eternity holds all endings and beginnings in the
completeness of his love, where the shimmering light of
timelessness renders powerless the ravages of time.

Daniel 7:13–14
Psalm 93
Revelation 1:5–8
John 18:33–37

*When Jesus looked up he saw some wealthy people putting their offerings into the treasury and he noticed a poor widow putting in two small coins. He said, "I tell you truly, this poor widow put in more than all the rest; for those others have all made offerings from their surplus wealth, but she, from her poverty, has offered her whole livelihood."*

—LUKE 21:1–4

Many years ago, when my daughter was just a toddler, she found me one day in tears. Before I could even pull myself together, she left the room and then came toddling in with her beloved teddy bear and placed it lovingly in my lap. It was all she had, and she gave it freely, and it meant more to me at that moment than all the wealth of nations.

Revelation 14:1–5
Psalm 24
Luke 21:1–4

# NOVEMBER 27

*All that you see here—the days will come when there will not be left a*
*stone upon another stone that will not be thrown down.*

—LUKE 21:6

What are these things we are "staring at" now? Are they
the bright lights of our must-have society or the ambitions
for wealth and reputation, or the many other things that
feed our lesser ego-selves? If so, the warning rings true.
These things will disintegrate in our hands even as we
clutch them. Maybe today we can spend some time fixing
our sight on all the qualities of God and of ourselves that
are lovely and eternal.

Revelation 14:14–19
Psalm 96
Luke 21:5–11

# NOVEMBER 28

*You will even be handed over by parents, brothers, relatives, and friends, and they will put some of you to death. You will be hated by all because of my name, but not a hair on your head will be destroyed. By your perseverance you will secure your lives.*

—LUKE 21:16–19

The purest light will reveal the darkest shadows. When we live true to the Christlight within us, the power of that light will provoke the darkness that lurks in human nature, and we will be called to follow, in our own small way, the path that leads to the cross. Betrayals will follow, Jesus warns us, and the worst betrayals will come from those we thought we most trusted: friends, family, and colleagues. The worst may happen, and yet Jesus promises life that transcends every cross.

Revelation 15:1–4
Psalm 98
Luke 21:12–19

# NOVEMBER 29

*Know that the LORD is God;*
*he made us, his we are;*
*his people, the flock he tends.*
—PSALM 100:3

There are many kinds of knowing. We can know
something in our heads: the facts of something, a narrative
we have been taught, the rules defining the way we are
supposed to live. And then there is the kind of knowing
that lodges in our gut and in our hearts. There is that
knowledge that we cherish of moments when God has
touched our innermost being, guiding us, opening our
eyes, and kindling a whole new level of life within us.
Today the psalmist urges us to know, in this deeper way,
who God is and who we are.

Revelation 18:1–2, 21–23; 19:1–3, 9
Psalm 100
Luke 21:20–28

*"Their voice has gone forth to all the earth,*
*and their words to the ends of the world."*

—ROMANS 10:18

For years Jim had been a much-loved speaker and teacher until throat cancer robbed him of what everyone considered God's most precious gift to him. I met him ten years later, long after conversation had become nearly impossible for him, and I knew as soon as I walked into his room that I was entering *presence*. Now all those who seek him are more enriched by this quiet holiness than they could be by wise words. Indeed, there is wisdom that transcends expression.

Romans 10:9–18
Psalm 19
Matthew 4:18–22

*An angel showed me the river of life-giving water, sparkling like crystal, flowing from the throne of God and of the Lamb down the middle of the street. On either side of the river grew the tree of life that produces fruit twelve times a year, once each month; the leaves of the trees serve as medicine for the nations.*

—REVELATION 22:1–2

The river of God's Spirit flows continually through the situations and circumstances of our lives. It strives toward life-in-all-its-fullness and longs to bring our hearts to fruitfulness and healing. That river asks only that we give our consent to its flow through our daily living. As we stand now, at the end of a year and the dawn of another Advent, let us offer our "Yes!" with hope and trust.

Revelation 22:1–7
Psalm 95
Luke 21:34–36

# DECEMBER 2

• FIRST SUNDAY OF ADVENT •

*The days are coming, says the LORD, when I will fulfill the promise*
*I made to the house of Israel and Judah.*

—JEREMIAH 33:14

"But Mom, you promised!" We all remember things we promised but never delivered. No doubt there were good reasons for our defaulting, but even so, it will have left a residue of disappointment, or even distrust, in its wake. By contrast, we hear today that God not only is going to deliver on his promise but also is going to fulfill it—to full and overflowing.

Jeremiah 33:14–16
Psalm 25
1 Thessalonians 3:12–4:2
Luke 21:25–28, 34–36

*In the days to come,*
*the mountain of the LORD's house*
*shall be established as the highest mountain*
*and raised above the hills.*
*All nations shall stream toward it;*
*many people shall come and say:*
*"Come, let us climb the LORD's mountain."*

—ISAIAH 2:2–3

The landscape of modern life contains great mountains of greed, empty valleys of need; mountains of ambition and success hiding wildernesses of failure and despair. Can we trust that the holy mountain of God truly eclipses them all, and that when we stand on its slopes we will see our mountains and valleys in a different perspective?

Isaiah 2:1–5
Psalm 122
Matthew 8:5–11

*Blessed are the eyes that see what you see. For I say to you, many prophets and kings desired to see what you see, but did not see it, and to hear what you hear, but did not hear it.*

—LUKE 10:23–24

What *do* you see? When you close your eyes and listen to the silence within you, do you see glimpses of the sacred moments when you truly felt that God had touched your life? Moments of guidance, insight, clarity, reassurance, courage, or calm? Such moments are packed with heart-knowledge that no one can deny or diminish. Remember them. Cherish them. Let them empower you.

Isaiah 11:1–10
Psalm 72
Luke 10:21–24

*On this mountain he will destroy
the veil that veils all peoples,
The web that is woven over all nations;
he will destroy death forever.*

—ISAIAH 25:7–8

When God removes the shrouds of death, we will discover
that they were swaddling clothes, not grave clothes, and
that our dying was actually a new birth.

Isaiah 25:6–10
Psalm 23
Matthew 15:29–37

*Everyone who listens to these words of mine and acts on them will be like a wise man who built his house on rock. The rain fell, the floods came, and the winds blew and buffeted the house. But it did not collapse; it had been set solidly on rock.*

—MATTHEW 7:24–25

A favorite picture of mine shows a lighthouse surrounded by wild and stormy seas. The lighthouse is swamped by the storm, but when the storm abates, the lighthouse still stands firm. I would rather my life were like that lighthouse, however storm battered, than like those sand castles I saw on the beach that the first rising tide will wash away.

Isaiah 26:1–6
Psalm 118
Matthew 7:21, 24–27

# DECEMBER 7

*When he entered the house, the blind men approached him and Jesus said to them, "Do you believe that I can do this?" "Yes, Lord," they said to him.*

—MATTHEW 9:28

A high-wire artist entertained people by pushing a wheelbarrow across a wire suspended high above a chasm. "Do you believe I can do this?" he called out to the spectators. "We do, we do!" they answered. "So, who is going to get in the wheelbarrow?" he asked. Do we believe in the power of God? Will we entrust ourselves to it entirely, against all the odds?

Isaiah 29:17–24
Psalm 27
Matthew 9:27–31

• THE IMMACULATE CONCEPTION OF THE BLESSED VIRGIN MARY •

*And behold, Elizabeth, your relative, has also conceived a son in her old age, and this is the sixth month for her who was called barren; for nothing will be impossible for God.*

—LUKE 1:36–37

God's power can completely derail our human plans and confound our expectations. If we can only trust this power working in us it can bring to fulfilment plans and dreams way beyond our imagination, and beyond anything we thought was possible.

Genesis 3:9–15, 20
Psalm 98
Ephesians 1:3–6, 11–12
Luke 1:26–38

# DECEMBER 9

*"Every valley shall be filled*
*and every mountain and hill shall be made low.*
*The winding roads shall be made straight,*
*and the rough ways made smooth."*

—LUKE 3:5

Jean had an average kind of a day as a grade-school teacher. She spent some time helping Jimmy smooth out the difficulties with his reading and chipped away a bit more of Mary's mountainous resistance to her arithmetic. She helped remove some of the practical problems that were troubling one student who had learning difficulties, and she worked with two other children to resolve a quarrel. She was preparing the way of the Lord, although she never realized it.

Baruch 5:1–9
Psalm 126
Philippians 1:4–6, 8–11
Luke 3:1–6

*Strengthen the hands that are feeble,*
*make firm the knees that are weak,*
*Say to those whose hearts are frightened:*
*Be strong, fear not!*

—ISAIAH 35:3–4

It's fear that makes our hands go limp when action is
needed and reduces our knees to jelly in the face of a
threat. It's fear that is the greatest block to our discipleship
and to our growth in God. No wonder, then, that God
addresses our fear directly.

Isaiah 35:1–10
Psalm 85
Luke 5:17–26

*Though the grass withers and the flower wilts,*
*the word of our God stands forever.*

—ISAIAH 40:8

The daffodils are so beautiful, but their springtime freshness lasts for only a few days, and then they wither and fade. The violets and daisies in the green grass sparkle in the morning sun, but by noon the gardener has passed through with the mower and they are gone. But the true life of the daffodil rests safe within the bulb and will always return. The true life of the violet and the daisy rests within the roots and will spring forth again and again.

Isaiah 40:1–11
Psalm 96
Matthew 18:12–14

*Sing and rejoice, O daughter Zion!*
*See, I am coming to dwell among you, says the LORD.*
—ZECHARIAH 2:14

Imagine that this were really to happen—the resurrected
Lord coming to your door and asking to live with you and
your family, in your neighborhood, among your friends.
What changes and reactions do you think that might
precipitate in your lifestyle and in your community?

Zechariah 2:14–17 or Revelation 11:19; 12:1–6, 10
Judith 13:18–19
Luke 1:26–38 or 1:39–47

# DECEMBER 13

• ST. LUCY, VIRGIN AND MARTYR •

*The afflicted and the needy seek water in vain,*
*their tongues are parched with thirst.*
*I, the LORD, will answer them;*
*I, the God of Israel, will not forsake them.*
*—ISAIAH 41:17*

We need only to switch on our television screen to see the
ones the prophet speaks of, reaching out desperate hands
for food and water. But whose hands will reach out to
answer them and satisfy their needs? Could it be our hands
the Lord requires? Will it be our hearts that either nourish
or abandon the thirsty?

Isaiah 41:13–20
Psalm 145
Matthew 11:11–15

*I, the LORD, your God,*
*teach you what is for your good,*
*and lead you on the way you should go.*
—ISAIAH 48:17

There are so many voices in my head telling me what to do. There is the voice of who I wish I were, or who I think I ought to be, or who I might have been in different circumstances. And there are the voices of friends, relatives, colleagues, and neighbors, all with their own ideas about how I should be. If I can silence the noise for a while and listen to the stirrings in my heart, I will hear a still, small voice—the voice of the Lord who knows who I am and where I should go.

Isaiah 48:17–19
Psalm 1
Matthew 11:16–19

*Take care of this vine,*
*and protect what your right hand has planted.*
—PSALM 80:15–16

In the vineyards of France, I first noticed the roses planted
at the ends of the long rows of vines. "The roses are there
to protect the vines," the guide told me. "If there is any
kind of blight, the roses show the damage first, and give us
an early warning, so that we can take measures to save the
vines." I gazed upon those beautiful, sacrificial roses, and
thought of Calvary.

Sirach 48:1–4, 9–11
Psalm 80
Matthew 17:9–13

*He will rejoice over you with gladness,*
*and renew you in his love,*
*he will sing joyfully because of you,*
*as one sings at festivals.*

—ZEPHANIAH 3:17–18

It had been a very long time since the friends had seen each other. They could hardly wait for the day of their reunion. When they finally met up, they were beside themselves with joy, and their joy renewed the love that had always united them. We recognize human love and joy with human eyes. Perhaps it takes a prophet's eyes to recognize God's love dancing for joy over *us*.

Zephaniah 3:14–18
Isaiah 12:2–6
Philippians 4:4–7
Luke 3:10–18

*O God, with your judgment endow the king,*
*and with your justice, the king's son;*
*He shall govern your people with justice*
*and your afflicted ones with judgment.*

—PSALM 72:2

It's a long inner journey from the human understanding of judgment as condemnation and punishment to a divine understanding of justice as the source of integrity and compassion. It's a long journey from the love of power to the power of love.

Genesis 49:2, 8–10
Psalm 72
Matthew 1:1–17

# DECEMBER 18

*"Behold, the virgin shall be with child and bear a son,*
*and they shall name him Emmanuel,"*
*which means "God is with us."*
—MATTHEW 1:23

God is with us, not remote from us.

God is with us, not against us.

God is with us when we think we are alone.

God is with us when our friends have quit.

God is with us when everything seems to be against us.

Emmanuel—what a promise! What a gift!

Jeremiah 23:5–8
Psalm 72
Matthew 1:18–25

⸺⸺⸺⸺⸺

*Be my rock of refuge,*
*a stronghold to give me safety,*
*for you are my rock and my fortress.*
—PSALM 71:3

At first my rock seems not to be solid at all. I find it in
the sea breeze at dawn, in the first spring flowers and the
colors of fall. My rock echoes back the song of the birds
and a child's laughter. All these things, and a million more,
bring me to stillness and remind me that whatever winds
are howling through my circumstances, the power of life
itself, the very breath of God, is an unfailing reality on
which I can build a life.

Judges 13:2–7, 24–25
Psalm 71
Luke 1:5–25

*"Hail, full of grace! The Lord is with you." But she was greatly troubled at what was said and pondered what sort of greeting this might be. Then the angel said to her, "Do not be afraid, Mary."*

—LUKE 1:28–30

The touch of God upon our lives will not be as dramatic as it was upon Mary's, but it is an invitation to bring forth in our own lives something of God's love. Just listen to the layers of emotion.

We are invited to Rejoice! Yet our response is more likely to express distress and disturbance and even terror that the living God has touched our hearts. And then, at the deepest level, is the utter consolation of the angel's words: "Don't be afraid." When we let go of the fear, the disturbance can turn into rejoicing.

Isaiah 7:10–14
Psalm 24
Luke 1:26–38

# DECEMBER 21

*Here he stands behind our wall,*
*gazing through the windows,*
*peering through the lattices.*
—SONG OF SONGS 2:9

The thought of a stranger standing behind the wall, peering in through the window, feels threatening. But this is no stranger. This is the One who loves us far more than we love ourselves or one another. God is watching for the slightest chink in our defenses, through which God's love might reach us, for the slightest hint that we might be ready to respond.

Song of Songs 2:8–14 or Zephaniah 3:14–18
Psalm 33
Luke 1:39–45

*I prayed for this child, and the LORD granted my request.
Now I, in turn, give him to the LORD; as long as he lives,
he shall be dedicated to the LORD.*

—1 SAMUEL 1:27–28

Hannah, in offering her child Samuel back to the Lord's
service, is also asking us a searching question: "What are
you praying for right now?" And if God answers our prayer
by granting what we long for, are we willing to give it
straight back to God, to be used for the service of God
and for the greater good of all God's creation?

1 Samuel 1:24–28
1 Samuel 2:1, 4–8
Luke 1:46–56

*Blessed are you who believed that what was spoken to you*
*by the Lord would be fulfilled.*

—LUKE 1:45

During Advent we hear of impossible events. The barren
Hannah brings Samuel to birth. The considerably
postmenopausal Elizabeth conceives John. The virgin
is found to be with child. They are three women who
believed the impossible and ran with it, accepting its
unforeseeable consequences. Blessed are they, indeed, for
believing what most of us would have dismissed out of
hand. Their belief nourishes and empowers our own.

Micah 5:1–4
Psalm 80
Hebrews 10:5–10
Luke 1:39–45

---

*You, my child, shall be called the prophet of the Most High,*
*for you will go before the Lord to prepare his way,*
*to give his people knowledge of salvation*
*by the forgiveness of their sins.*

—LUKE 1:76

This message, to the newborn John, is a message to each
of us: What is the least self-important, the most vulnerable,
and the most receptive, will become the gateway through
which our souls will find their way to God.

2 Samuel 7:1–5, 8–12, 14, 16
Psalm 89
Luke 1:67–79

# DECEMBER 25

• THE NATIVITY OF THE LORD • CHRISTMAS •

*Let us go, then, to Bethlehem to see this thing that has taken place,*
*which the Lord has made known to us.*

—LUKE 2:15

God is coming to birth in a million ways, in a million places, today. God is coming to birth in your neighborhood, in the family around you, in the ones you are aching for, and in the ones you are rejoicing over. Take a moment to discover for yourself this thing that is happening. Where do you discover Bethlehem on this most holy day?

| **Vigil:** | **Dawn:** |
|:---:|:---:|
| Isaiah 62:1–5 | Isaiah 62:11–12 |
| Psalm 89 | Psalm 97 |
| Acts 13:16–17, 22–25 | Titus 3:4–7 |
| Matthew 1:1–25 or 1:18–25 | Luke 2:15–20 |
| **Midnight:** | **Day:** |
| Isaiah 9:1–6 | Isaiah 52:7–10 |
| Psalm 96 | Psalm 98 |
| Titus 2:11–14 | Hebrews 1:1–6 |
| Luke 2:1–14 | John 1:1–18 or 1:1–5, 9–14 |

# DECEMBER 26

• ST. STEPHEN, THE FIRST MARTYR •

*Into your hands I commend my spirit;*
*you will redeem me, O LORD, O faithful God. . . .*
*I will rejoice and be glad because of your mercy.*

—PSALM 31:5–6, 8

The joy of Christmas is followed very quickly by a
reminder of the cost of discipleship. When we choose to
follow the Holy Child, we will experience his cross, each
in our own way. Stephen shows us, today, how to embrace
whatever opposition we meet with the trust and faith that
we can surrender entirely into God's hands and never stop
rejoicing in God's love.

Acts 6:8–10, 7:54–59
Psalm 31
Matthew 10:17–22

---

*On the first day of the week, Mary Magdalene ran and went to Simon Peter and to the other disciple whom Jesus loved.*

—JOHN 20:2

Hope and faith, courage and persistence—all of these can help us live more fully and face death more confidently. But only love can carry us through and beyond death to the joy of a life that is eternal.

1 John 1:1–4
Psalm 97
John 20:1–8

*Joseph rose and took the child and his mother by night and departed for Egypt. He stayed there until the death of Herod.*

— MATTHEW 2:14–15

The trek to asylum in Egypt continues in every displaced migrant family in our world today and will do so until the Herod of our violent ways is dead. May the light that made Bethlehem radiant guide them to safe havens and enlighten the hearts and minds of all our Herods.

1 John 1:5–2:2
Psalm 124
Matthew 2:13–18

*Lord, now let your servant go in peace;*
*your word has been fulfilled:*
*My own eyes have seen the salvation*
*which you prepared in the sight*
*of every people.*
—LUKE 2:29–31

This prayer, first spoken by Simeon, is often used as a night prayer. Can *we* say, each evening, as we reflect on everything the day has brought, the people, the incidents, the moments, and the hours, "Yes! Today my eyes, too, have glimpsed the presence and the power of God that one day all the nations shall know and recognize?"

1 John 2:3–11
Psalm 96
Luke 2:22–35

# DECEMBER 30

*He went down with them and came to Nazareth, and was obedient to them; and his mother kept all these things in her heart. And Jesus advanced in wisdom and age and favor before God and man.*

—LUKE 2:51–52

He whose power commands the heavens and the earth consents to live under human authority. He whose love fills all eternity surrenders to the processes of human growth and development. May we learn from his humility. May we, also, grow in wisdom and grace.

Sirach 3:2–6, 12–14, or 1 Samuel 1:20–22, 24–28
Psalm 128
Colossians 3:12–21 or 3:12–17 or 1 John 3:1–2, 21–24
Luke 2:41–52

*Sing to the LORD a new song;*
*sing to the LORD, all you lands.*
*Sing to the LORD; bless his name;*
*announce his salvation, day after day.*
—PSALM 96:1–2

Every new day a new song! May this new year that begins
at midnight become a year in which all our songs find their
fulfillment in the perfect symphony of God.

1 John 2:18–21
Psalm 96
John 1:1–18